GE
FRO
THE
ORIGINAL

BY HAROLD J. BERRY

BACK TO THE BIBLE
A Publication

75¢

order from

Back to the Bible Broadcast

Box 82808   Lincoln, Nebraska 68501

12,000 printed to date—1972
(5-1743—12M—122)

Printed in the United States of America

Foreword

God, in His infinite wisdom, used Alexander the Great to bring about the universality of the Greek language. This language, with its fine shades of meaning, was then used by God as He inspired the New Testament writings, which could be understood by the common man of that time. Those today who do not know New Testament Greek can praise the Lord for those who have studied it and who seek to communicate its meaning to others.

Realizing the need for people to understand the marvelous depths of the New Testament, the *Good News Broadcaster* began a column entitled Gems From the Original, written by Harold J. Berry.

The purpose was not to give an exhaustive treatment of any particular problem but to show the riches of the Greek New Testament and to provide spiritual food and help to those who study the Bible.

Many readers found this column to be very helpful and asked to have the articles put in book form. This book is the result. Each chapter was a separate article when the material appeared in the *Good News Broadcaster*. We are pleased to give these articles a wider distribution by now publishing them in book form.

—Theodore H. Epp

Contents

Chapter 1

The Believer's Old Nature

Inasmuch as the New Testament was first written in the Greek language, it is especially intriguing to go back beyond our translations to see some of the fine shades of meaning of the original words. Rarely does the proper use of the Greek word completely change the meaning that we have in our translations, but it often makes the thought more forceful and draws the doctrinal distinctions even finer.

Such a word is *katargeo*, which appears 27 times in the Greek New Testament. It is translated various ways in the King James Version. Five times it is translated by the word "destroy," four times by the words "done away," three times by the word "abolish," twice by the words "make of none effect" and once each by 13 other words.

The basic meaning of *katargeo* is "to make idle or inactive." It is also used in the sense of "to render inoperative"—or as we might say it, "to put out of commission."

This word occurs once in Luke, and all other occurrences are in Paul's epistles (if you consider Hebrews, where it appears once, to be from his pen). One of the most crucial places it occurs is

Romans 6:6 where it is translated "destroyed": "Knowing this, that our old man is crucified with him, that the body of sin might be destroyed, that henceforth we should not serve sin." A proper understanding of the word is essential in this passage if one is to know the true relationship of the old nature in the Christian's life. There are two extremes of Christian thinking involved: some think the old nature still has such a death grip on them that they cannot effectively serve Christ, and some think the old nature was completely eradicated when they received Christ and that they no longer sin at all.

An examination of some other passages in which the word occurs will help us to understand its true force in Romans 6:6. In Luke 13:7 the word is translated "cumbereth": "Then said he unto the dresser of his vineyard, Behold, these three years I come seeking fruit on this fig tree, and find none: cut it down; why cumbereth it the ground?" It is obvious in this parable that the fig tree had not destroyed the ground but was only taking up space and making the ground idle when it could have been productive.

The same word is translated "without effect" in Romans 3:3, where the apostle asks, "For what if some did not believe? shall their unbelief make the faith [faithfulness] of God without effect?" The thought here is that just because some people do not believe in God, this does not negate His faithfulness. Paul states the same truth another way in II Timothy 2:13: "If we believe not, yet he abideth faithful: he cannot deny himself."

Another interesting verse that uses the word *katargeo* is I Corinthians 13:8, where this one word is translated both "fail" and "vanish away." Paul said, "Charity [love] never faileth: but whether there be prophecies, they shall fail; whether there be tongues, they shall cease; whether there be knowledge, it shall vanish away."

Contention had arisen in the Corinthian church over gifts. This church did not lack any of the gifts (1:7), and yet the believers were not spiritual but carnal (3:1). In I Corinthians 13 Paul was instructing the believers in the proper way to use their gifts—in love. In order to establish the superiority of love, the apostle reminded them that there would come a time when the gifts of prophecy and knowledge would be rendered inoperative, but love will always continue in its importance. Verse 10 of this same passage affirms that "when that which is perfect is come, then that which is in part shall be done away." Here the word *katargeo* is translated "done away." That which is in part is not destroyed, but it is no longer necessary when that which is complete is present.

In light of the above, it is evident in Romans 6 that the sin nature was not destroyed in the sense that we normally use the word, but rather it was rendered inoperative. It is like a radio that is unplugged; it is not destroyed, but its power has been broken. Though the power of the old nature over the believer is broken, he is still able to put it back into operation by yielding to its desires.

The conflict within every believer, therefore, is whether to yield to the new nature he has because he is in Christ or to the old nature with its self-desires. In Galatians 5:16 Paul said, "Walk in the Spirit, and ye shall not fulfil the lust of the flesh."

The believer is to yield to the Spirit, not to the flesh. When the believer commits an act of sin, he breaks his fellowship with the Spirit. The believer's remedy for broken fellowship is found in I John 1:9: "If we confess our sins, he is faithful and just to forgive us our sins, and to cleanse us from all unrighteousness." When the Christian confesses his sin, God forgives his disobedience, and once again the fruit of the Spirit is manifested through his life. Yielding to the desires of the flesh will result in the manifestation of the works of the flesh, but walking by means of the Spirit will result in the manifestation of the fruit of the Spirit.

The person who has received Christ as Saviour is no longer in bondage to the power of the old nature. Christ broke the power of sin through his death on the cross. Though each believer is delivered from the power of sin, he is still capable of sinning by choosing to yield to the desires of the flesh. All believers may look forward to that day when Christ will return to deliver His own from the very presence of sin by taking them to be with Himself.

Chapter 2

'Power': Ability or Authority?

There are six words in the Greek New Testament that are translated "power" in various English translations. The two principal words are *dunamis* and *exousia*. Although the word "power" is not necessarily a bad translation for either of these words, it is at least obvious that since they are different words, they must emphasize different aspects of power. When you learn the special emphasis of each word, the New Testament will take on an even richer meaning for you as you search out the truths of God's Word.

Dunamis occurs 120 times in the Greek New Testament. In the King James Version this word is translated "strength" 7 times, "miracle" 8 times, "mighty work" 11 times, and "power" 77 times. Other translations of this word are mostly one-time occurrences. From this it is seen that by far the most common translation of this word is "power." But power in what sense?

"Power" may be used in speaking of a football player who is a rock-hard 200 pounds and is able to drive through the middle of the defensive line. Or "power" may be used to convey the idea of authority—a policeman has power because he has authority invested in him by his government, but his power is not greater than the authority given to him by his superiors.

The word *dunamis* is power in the sense of "ability," though it does not always stress this aspect of power. In II Corinthians 8:3 the word *dunamis* is used to emphasize ability: "For to their power, I bear record, yea, and beyond their power they were willing of themselves." The Corinthians gave of their finances according to their ability or means after they had first given themselves to the Lord. Their power to give was their ability to give.

The word *dunamis* is also used in the New Testament in assuring the Christian that God is responsible for keeping him: "Who are kept by the power of God through faith unto salvation ready to be revealed in the last time" (I Pet. 1:5). While it is true that God has the authority to keep the Christian secure because He has all authority, yet what is stressed in this verse is that the believer is kept by the ability of God. Because God is omnipotent, the believer never needs to be concerned that God may not have enough ability to keep him secure.

Perhaps one of the most significant verses where *dunamis* occurs as far as the Christian is concerned is Acts 1:8: "But ye shall receive power, after that the Holy Ghost is come upon you: and ye shall be witnesses unto me both in Jerusalem, and in all Judaea, and in Samaria, and unto the uttermost part of the earth." Christ assured the believers that they would have power to witness after the Holy Spirit came into their lives. While it is true that the believer can witness with authority because he knows Christ as Saviour, the greatest concern voiced by the average Christian is that he might have the ability to witness. Because Acts 1:8 uses the word *dunamis* for "power," it is clear that Christ was stressing to the believers that the *ability* to witness would be theirs after the coming of the Holy Spirit into their lives.

A synonym for *dunamis* is the word *exousia*, which appears 104 times in the Greek New Testament. *Exousia* is translated "authority" 29 times and "power" 69 times. Therefore, it is evident that the word "power" is the most common translation for both *dunamis* and *exousia*. While *dunamis* frequently stresses the matter of ability, *exousia* stresses authority or right. The primary meaning of *exousia* is the "power of choice" or "liberty of action." Hence, in New Testament times it was commonly used in wills and contracts to denote the "claim" or "right" that one had over something.

The primary meaning of *exousia* is seen in I Corinthians 9:6: "Or I only and Barnabas, have not we power to forbear working?" It is obvious in this verse that the Apostle Paul was talking about his authority or right to make the decision not to work. Since he and Barnabas were giving their lives to minister to others, they could expect to be supported by those to whom they were ministering. Paul had the authority to make this decision, but he chose to support himself by his own labors so that the gospel could be preached without charge.

The word *exousia* is also used in Romans 9:21: "Hath not the potter power over the clay, of the same lump to make one vessel unto honour, and another unto dishonour?" Here it is evident that the potter has the right to decide what he will do with the clay—he has the authority to choose.

One of the most commonly quoted verses where *exousia* appears is John 1:12: "But as many as received him, to them gave he power to become the sons of God, even to them that believe on his name." It is extremely significant that *exousia*, which stresses right or authority, is used in John 1:12 and not *dunamis*, which emphasizes the ability or means to do something. The Scriptures make it clear that no one has the ability in himself to become a child of God, because it is impossible to merit salvation through works: "For by grace are ye saved through faith; and that not of yourselves: it is the gift of God: not of works, lest any man should boast" (Eph. 2:8,9). However, the good news is that even though you cannot earn salvation by works, it is your right by the power of choice to become a child of God by receiving Jesus Christ as your personal Saviour. This authority is given to you by Jesus Christ Himself, because when you receive Him as Saviour, the righteousness of God is imputed or placed on your account so that you have a perfect position in Christ. This is not because of your ability but because of what Christ accomplished for you on the cross.

How thrilling it is not only to be children of God by the power of choice but also to have the ability to witness to others as a result of the indwelling Holy Spirit in our lives.

Chapter 3

'Sin': Habitual or Occasional?

Some of the greatest benefits to be reaped from a knowledge of New Testament Greek result from a proper understanding of the tenses. Greek tenses are more complex than English tenses.

In English the tense of a verb has to do only with the time of the action—past, present or future. In the Greek language there are two important factors in every tense: the time of the action (as in English), and the kind of action. The kind of action is often more important than the time of the action.

The Greek tenses are able to show such things as present continuous action, past continuous action, past complete action with a continuing effect, past action viewed in a single perspective without reference to the limits of the action, and future action that is either continuous or viewed in a single perspective.

All these tenses and their fine shades of meaning are important, and this is especially true of the present tense. In fact, it is impossible to understand some passages in the New Testament unless one understands the significance of the present tense. This is particularly true of I John 3:6-9.

The Greek present tense emphasizes continuous action in present time. When the Bible student realizes which verbs are in the present tense in I John 3:6-9, he is amazed at how easily an otherwise difficult passage can be understood. Verse 6 says, "Whosoever abideth in him sinneth not: whosoever sinneth hath not seen him, neither known him." The verb "sinneth," used twice in this verse, is in the present tense. Since the present tense emphasizes continuous action, it is evident that this verse is talking about the person who continually sins. Therefore, the one who habitually sins is not abiding in Christ; that is, he has not received Christ as his Saviour.

There are those who say this verse teaches that if a person sins at all, it is evident he is not a child of God. But this verse does not support such teaching. The First Epistle of John was written to show Christians the importance of fellowship and to point out the marks of a true Christian. In verse 1 of chapter 2, the Apostle John reminded Christians that he wrote these things "that ye sin not." But note that he added, "And if any man sin, we have an advocate with the Father, Jesus Christ the righteous." Although John was writing to help Christians live free from sin, he was aware that they might fall into occasional acts of sin; therefore, he reminded them that Christ was standing by, ready to be their Heavenly Advocate if they should happen to sin. This assurance was especially meaningful because John had just told his readers, "If we confess our sins, he is faithful and just to forgive us our sins, and to cleanse us from all unrighteousness" (1:9).

John also gave this assurance: "Little children, let no man deceive you: he that doeth righteousness is righteous, even as he is righteous" (3:7). In this verse the word "doeth" is in the present tense. Therefore, the verse stresses that the result of one's being a Christian is that he practices righteousness; it is impossible for anyone to habitually do righteous acts unless he is a Christian. When a person receives Christ, the Holy Spirit indwells his life and works out the life of Christ through him. This results in practicing righteousness.

Verse 8 further develops this thought: "He that committeth sin is of the devil; for the devil sinneth from the beginning." Here the verbs "committeth" and "sinneth" are both in the present tense, which emphasizes continual action.

From verse 6 we learned that whoever practices sin has not known Christ; in verse 8 we discover that such a person really has his origin in the Devil. This is never said of a person after he receives Christ as Saviour, even though he is capable of committing occasional acts of sin. The one who has placed his faith in Christ has been born again, and his origin is no longer in Satan but in Christ.

Since his fall it has been in Satan's nature to practice sin; but the last part of verse 8 reminds us, "For this purpose the Son of God was manifested, that he might destroy the works of the devil."

Verse 9 states one of the most profound truths in the New Testament: "Whosoever is born of God doth not commit sin." It is impossible to properly interpret this phrase without an awareness of the significance of the Greek present tense—continuous action in present time. The verb "commit" is in the present tense. This verse does not say that a person who is born of God never commits occasional acts of sin, but it does teach that a person who is born of God will not practice sin throughout his life.

The question that naturally arises is, How is it possible to make such an absolute statement about the Christian? The answer is given in the rest of the verse: "For his [God's] seed remaineth in him: and he cannot sin, because he is born of God." The verb "remaineth" is also in the present tense. Why is it impossible for a true believer to practice sin, or to habitually sin? Because God's seed continually remains in him.

This is why God can trust the believer to live, without giving him a set of laws such as the Mosaic Law. The believer has the righteousness of God credited to him, so he no longer desires to sin. He wants to please God in every aspect; and when he does commit sin, the Holy Spirit convicts him of it. The significant difference between a saved person who sins and an unsaved person who sins is that the saved person is convicted by the indwelling Holy Spirit, but the unsaved person is not.

It is wonderful to realize that when a person receives Christ, he becomes a new creature, and the old things pass away (II Cor. 5:17). Therefore, the born-again person no longer habitually does those things that dishonor God, because the indwelling Holy Spirit has changed his desires.

Chapter 4

'Reprove': Accuse or Convict?

Every believer ought to be concerned about how he can have a more effective witness to the unsaved people around him. It is not methods, logic or rhetoric that actually bring a person to Christ, but rather it is the Holy Spirit—He produces the new birth (John 3:5,6). It is obvious, then, that if any Christian is to be successful in introducing others to Christ, he must know how the Holy Spirit works in lives to bring conviction of sin and a desire to know Christ as Saviour.

One of the most significant passages in the Bible that give insight into the working of the Holy Spirit in salvation is John 16:7-11. In this passage, which is a part of the "upper room discourse," Christ tells the disciples that after He has ascended to the Father, He will send another Comforter, or Paraclete, who will be of help to them. This reference is to the Holy Spirit, who descended at Pentecost to take up residence in the life of every believer. Christ promised that when the Holy Spirit came, He would reprove the world of sin, of righteousness and of judgment (v. 8).

But what is it to "reprove" the world of these things? To reprove or rebuke does not necessarily

19

mean to convince people they are wrong. A parent may reprove his teenager for staying out too late at night, but this doesn't mean the young person is really convinced it was wrong. And it is also possible to unjustly rebuke a person when he is really not guilty.

The extent of the Spirit's work is understood from John 16:7-11 when one learns the true meaning of the word "reprove." This word is a translation of the Greek word, *elegcho*, which appears 17 times in the New Testament. In six of its occurrences this word is translated "reprove"; five times it is translated "rebuke"; four times, "convince"; once, "convict"; and once, "tell one's fault."

As *elegcho* was used in New Testament times, it involved conviction that was based on unquestionable proof. It was used in the courts of the day when referring to a person who had been tried and convicted. This word stresses conviction to the extent that there is no doubt in the person's mind but that the one on trial is guilty.

In New Testament usage Christ brought out the force of this word by applying it to Himself. He asked, "Which of you convinceth me of sin?" (John 8:46). The word translated "convinceth" is the word *elegcho*. Since this word means "to convict or convince," Christ was able to say that no one convicted Him of sin, obviously because He had no sin.

On the basis of the true meaning of *elegcho* we see that the Holy Spirit will actually convict, or convince, the world of sin, righteousness and judgment. It is not that He rebukes and the person remains unconvinced; rather, it is a convincing of the individual of sin, of righteousness and of judgment.

The question logically arises as to what sin is referred to in this passage. This sin is specified in John 16:9: "Of sin, because they believe not on me." The sin involved is not various acts of wrongdoing but failure to believe in Jesus Christ.

As we witness to others, we need to emphasize that the reason they are under condemnation is not because of individual habits but because they have refused to place their faith in Jesus Christ as their personal Saviour.

Christ also promised that the Holy Spirit would convict the world of righteousness. Not only is it the Spirit's ministry to convince the unsaved person of his sin, He also convinces him that the righteousness of God will be applied to him if he will place his faith in Christ. The unsaved person will probably not be able to express what has happened in this way, but it is the work of the Spirit to convince him that he will be acceptable to God if he places his faith in Christ.

The Holy Spirit also convicts the unsaved of judgment. Notice it is not of the judgment that is coming but of a judgment that is past, for it is the judgment of the "prince of this world" (v. 11). The words "is judged" (v. 11) should literally be "has been judged." The "prince of this world" refers to the same person that II Corinthians 4:4 calls the "god of this world." This person is Satan. He has blinded the minds of the unsaved. Satan was judged when Christ died on the cross, though the time of his final execution is yet to come. It is the ministry of the Holy Spirit to convince the unsaved person that sin has been judged at the cross and

21

that he can escape condemnation by placing his faith in Christ.

In light of these truths in John 16:7-11, the Christian can do no better in his witnessing than to help the unsaved person see what the Holy Spirit is bringing him to see: that he is condemned for his rejection of Jesus Christ, that the righteousness of God will be given to him when he believes (II Cor. 5:21), and that his sin has been judged on the cross and he can have eternal life by receiving Christ as Saviour.

Chapter 5

Binding What Is Already Bound

After Peter's confession, "Thou art the Christ, the Son of the living God" (Matt. 16:16), Christ said, "I will give unto thee the keys of the kingdom of heaven: and whatsoever thou shalt bind on earth shall be bound in heaven: and whatsoever thou shalt loose on earth shall be loosed in heaven" (v. 19).

Almost the identical statement was made to the other disciples (Matt. 18:18), so it is obvious that more than Peter were included in this promise. But what is really meant by this statement that has confused so many? In what sense is it true that whatever Peter and the other disciples bound would also be bound in heaven? Does this mean that they had the authority to forgive sin as well as not to forgive sin?

The solution lies in the proper understanding of the Greek tense used in the words "be bound" and "be loosed." In the discussion of the Greek tenses in chapter 3 it was stressed that there are two factors involved in each Greek tense: the time of the action and the kind of action. As to the time of the action, the Greek perfect tense denotes past time. As to the kind of action, this tense sees it as completed action with continuing effect.

The perfect tense is used in Galatians 2:20, where Paul says, "I am crucified with Christ." Literally, it is, "I have been crucified with Christ." The apostle had already been crucified with Christ because he had previously received Him as Saviour. His crucifixion with Christ was a past act, but it had a continuing effect on his life.

The perfect tense is also used in Ephesians 2:8, which says, "For by grace are ye saved." Literally, it is, "For by grace you have been saved." The Ephesian Christians had already been saved by the time of Paul's writing to them, and the effect of their conversion had continued in their lives.

With the significance of the Greek perfect tense in mind, the solution to the problem presented in Matthew 16:19 is not difficult to find. The words "be bound" and "be loosed" are in the Greek perfect tense, but this translation does not adequately convey the true force of this tense. Literally, it is "Whatever you bind on earth shall already have been bound in heaven, and whatever you loose on earth shall already have been loosed in heaven."

In light of this, what is the meaning intended in Matthew 16:19 and 18:18? Is it not meaningless to bind what is already bound and to loose what is already loosed? There is some support for the idea of understanding the words "bind" and "loose" to be common in rabbinical language for "forbid" and "permit." If this is intended, the meaning would be that the disciples were to forbid on earth what was already forbidden in heaven and to permit on earth what was already permitted in heaven.

24

It is perhaps most logical from the context to take the meaning to be that the disciples had the responsibility and privilege of telling others what was true of them as far as God was concerned. The person who refused to place his trust in Christ was still bound by sin, but the person who received Him as Saviour was loosed from the bondage of sin. Every Christian can exercise this same prerogative today. If a person has received Christ as Saviour, we can assure him he is loosed from sin, because he has already been loosed as far as God is concerned; and we can declare those bound who refuse Christ, because this is already true from God's viewpoint.

These truths also apply to John 20:23, which says, "Whose soever sins ye remit [forgive], they are remitted [forgiven] unto them; and whose soever sins ye retain, they are retained." The words "are remitted" and "are retained" are in the perfect tense. Therefore, the meaning of this verse is similar to Matthew 16:19; 18:18. The disciples could declare sins forgiven only if they had already been forgiven in heaven. And they could refuse to forgive the sins of those who had rejected Christ only because in heaven their sins were still unforgiven.

No one but God has the power to forgive sin, and He has never given this power to any man. If any person claims to have this power, he should be reminded that not only is there no scriptural basis for such a claim, this is a false gospel and the curse of God rests on that person: "If any man preach any other gospel unto you than that ye have received, let him be accursed" (Gal. 1:9).

What a wonderful privilege it is to tell others about Christ and to tell them they can be loosed from sin's penalty by receiving Christ as Saviour!

Chapter 6

Which Hell Is Eternal?

Much confusion about hell has resulted from the fact that three Greek words are translated by the same English word in the King James Version. The three Greek words are *tartaros*, *hades* and *geenna*, which are all translated "hell." When most people think of the word "hell," they think of the final destiny of those who reject Christ as Saviour. But do all three of these words refer to that place?

The word *tartaros* occurs only once in the New Testament: "God spared not the angels that sinned, but cast them down to hell, and delivered them into chains of darkness, to be reserved unto judgment" (II Pet. 2:4). The word "hell" in this verse is a translation of a verb form of *tartaros;* namely, *tartarosas*, "he was cast down to hell." The individuals involved in II Peter 2:4 were not those who had rejected Christ; rather, they were angels who had sinned and who are now reserved for judgment. Therefore, *tartaros* does not refer to "hell" as we commonly think of it; rather, it refers to a place of confinement for these angels until they are judged.

The word *hades* occurs ten times in the New Testament. It is used by three authors: Matthew,

Luke and John. The word appears twice in Matthew (11:23; 16:18), twice in Luke (10:15; 16:23), twice in Acts (2:27,31), and four times in Revelation (1:18; 6:8; 20:13,14). A detailed study of the context of each of these verses provides interesting information about *hades*, but perhaps the most information in one passage is found in Luke 16:19-31. Questions about what it is like in *hades* are answered in this passage.

The rich man in *hades* still retained his senses, for he was fully conscious of the torment through which he was passing. Not only could he feel the torment of *hades* itself, he was tormented by the thought that his five brothers yet at home would also come to this place. He thought he could prevent them from coming to *hades* if he could persuade Abraham to send Lazarus to talk to them. But Abraham reminded him that if his five brothers would not pay any attention to Moses and the prophets, they would not be persuaded even if someone who had risen from the dead went to them.

It is obvious that the rich man in *hades* was not experiencing what some cults refer to as "soul sleep," the supposed unconscious existence of the dead prior to the resurrection of the body. The rich man had all of his faculties and was experiencing extreme torment.

Though there is torment, *hades* is only a temporary abode for dead unbelievers. Revelation 20:13-15 says that *hades* (translated "hell") will deliver up the dead which is in it, and these people will be judged and then cast into the lake of fire. In light of this, *hades* is not the final destiny of those who reject Christ, but it is a place of torment for

28

them until they are resurrected to stand before God at the Great White Throne Judgment. Since *hades* is not the final destiny of the lost, *"hades"* is another word that does not fit the teaching regarding the place we commonly refer to as "hell."

The other word translated "hell" is *geenna*. This word occurs 12 times in the New Testament and is used by 4 authors—Matthew, Mark, Luke and James. *Geenna* occurs seven times in Matthew (5:22,29,30; 10:28; 18:9; 23:15,33), three times in Mark (9:43,45,47), once in Luke (12:5), and once in James (3:6).

Six of the twelve references to *geenna* mention fire as one of its characteristics. Eleven of the twelve references are in the Gospels and are the recorded words of the Lord Jesus Christ. But where did the word *geenna* come from?

Southeast of Jerusalem there was a valley known as the "valley of the son of Hinnom" (Josh. 15:8). It was also referred to as "Gehenna" from the Hebrew word, *ge-hinnom*, which means "valley of Hinnom." During Old Testament times children were offered to Molech in this valley (II Chron. 33:1-6; Jer. 7:31).

Later, after such heathen practices were stopped, the Jews used the valley to dispose of their rubbish as well as the bodies of dead animals and unburied criminals. To consume all of this, a fire burned continuously, known as the "Gehenna of fire." To be in the "Gehenna of fire" would be the most excruciating torment the human mind could imagine; thus, Christ used this well-known place, with its gnawing worms and burning fires, to

29

teach truths about the unknown place—the final abode of those who reject Him as Saviour.

In Mark 9:42-50 Christ emphasized that it would be better to lose the most precious things in this life and avoid hell than it would be to retain all that this life holds dear and be cast into hellfire, "where their worm dieth not, and the fire is not quenched" (vv. 44,46,48).

Geenna is also referred to as the "lake of fire" (Rev. 20:15). Verses 11-15 tell about the Great White Throne Judgment, and here we see that "death" (where the body has gone) and *hades* (where the soul has gone) will give up the dead that are in them. The resurrected unbelievers will then stand before the Great White Throne to be judged according to their works.

This judgment will not be for salvation, because that will already have been decided. It is because these have rejected Christ that they will stand before the Great White Throne. Apparently this judgment will determine the degree of punishment the unbelievers must endure during their never-ending state of existence. After the judgment, the unbelievers will be cast into the "lake of fire." This is the place Christ had referred to as *geenna*.

Unbelievers are not consumed or annihilated in the lake of fire. This fact is seen by comparing Revelation 19:20 with 20:10. Before the beginning of the 1000-year rule of Christ, two persons known as the "beast" and "false prophet" will be cast into the lake of fire. After the 1000-year rule of Christ, Satan will also be cast into the lake of fire, and the beast and false prophet will still be there. The unbeliever's punishment for rejecting Christ is spoken of as "everlasting punishment" (Matt. 25:46). Thus, *geenna*, not *tartaros* or *hades*, refers to the eternal hell.

There are those who object to the teaching about hell, saying that this is not compatible with the biblical teaching about God's love. Since He is a God of love, they argue, it would be impossible for Him to send anyone to such a place.

It is true that Matthew 25:41 says the "everlasting fire" was prepared for the Devil and his angels. But this same verse makes it clear that people will also be cast into this place. The context refers to the judgment of the living Gentiles, and verse 46 shows that the destiny of the unbelievers will be "everlasting punishment." Since verse 46 also mentions "life eternal," one cannot logically deny "everlasting punishment" without also denying "life eternal." The words "everlasting" and "eternal" are simply different translations of the same Greek word.

God is holy and cannot compromise His standards. He is also just and requires that sin must be dealt with. Man's willful sin has separated him from God and has brought him under God's condemnation. Without the intervention of a loving God, no one would be saved from eternal condemnation. But because He is a God of love and is not willing that any should perish (II Pet. 3:9), God sent His only begotten Son to die for the sins of the world (I John 2:2). Those who receive Christ as Saviour are delivered from all condemnation (John 5:24), but those who reject Him will continue in their condemnation throughout all eternity in the lake of fire. Have you received Christ as your Saviour?

"For God so loved the world, that he gave his only begotten Son, that whosoever believeth in him should not perish, but have everlasting life. For God sent not his Son into the world to condemn the world; but that the world through him might be saved. He that believeth on him is not condemned: but he that believeth not is condemned already, because he hath not believed in the name of the only begotten Son of God" (John 3:16-18).

Chapter 7

'Temple': Sacred Place or Inner Sanctuary?

There is a very careful distinction drawn in the Scriptures between the Greek words translated "temple." A knowledge of which word is used in a given passage allows some interesting observations to be made about the significance of the events involved.

The Greek word *hieron* refers to the entire precincts of the temple, including the outer courts, the porches, and other buildings which were connected with the temple itself. *Hieron* is used 71 times in the New Testament and always refers to a literal temple. The word is never used in a figurative sense, such as applying it to a person. The word is used almost exclusively in the New Testament to refer to the temple at Jerusalem, although it was also used to refer to the temple of Diana (Acts 19:27). This shows that there is nothing spiritual in the word itself, as it could be applied to both the temple of the true God and to the temples of heathen deities. The significance of the word is that it refers to that which is consecrated to deity; therefore, it would refer to the entire temple area regardless of the temple involved.

The other Greek word translated "temple" in the New Testament is *naos*. This word refers to the inner sanctuary as distinct from the whole temple enclosure. *Naos* is used 46 times in the New Testament. Once it is translated "shrine," and 45 times it is translated "temple." *Naos* comes from a word which means "to inhabit." Therefore, as a noun it refers to the inhabited place. Thus, as far as the Jerusalem temple was concerned, *naos* was applied to the Holy Place and the Holy of Holies, which composed the inner sanctuary of the temple. These areas were reserved for the priests alone—no one else could enter. The priests could minister in the Holy Place, but only the high priest could minister in the Holy of Holies—and then only once a year. How sacred the inner sanctuary was to God is indicated by the precise instructions He gave concerning it.

On the basis of the distinction between these two words for "temple," much light is thrown on several passages. In Luke 1 we read that Zacharias went "into the temple [*naos*] of the Lord" (v. 9) to burn incense and that the people remained "without" (v. 10). The people were obviously in the temple area (*hieron*), but were outside the inner sanctuary (*naos*) where Zacharias was burning incense.

It is also mentioned in the Scriptures that Christ taught in the temple (Matt. 26:55; Mark 12:35; Luke 19:47). The word used for "temple" in these verses is *hieron;* it is not *naos*, which would be the inner sanctuary. During His lifetime on earth, Christ was never permitted into the *naos*, or inner sanctuary, for only those who were priests were permitted there. The priests were of the tribe of Levi, but Christ was born of the tribe of Judah and thus would have been excluded from the inner sanctuary of the temple. This gives us a further glimpse into Christ's humility, as portrayed in Philippians 2. Christ was willing not only to give up the outward manifestation of His attributes but also to be born into a tribe that would exclude Him from the inner sanctuary of the temple, which was inhabited by God. He was willing to be excluded from the special presence of God on earth.

Distinguishing between the two words for "temple" also helps one to have further insights into the hopelessness and disdain for spiritual things that Judas had. Judas covenanted with the chief priests to deliver Jesus to them for 30 pieces of silver. After Jesus had been betrayed and turned over to Pontius Pilate, Judas "repented himself, and brought again the thirty pieces of silver to the chief priests and elders, saying, I have sinned in that I have betrayed the innocent blood. And they said, What is that to us? see thou to that. And he cast down the pieces of silver in the temple [*naos*], and departed, and went and hanged himself" (Matt. 27:3-5). Judas threw the 30 pieces of silver into the *naos*, the inner sanctuary, where only the priests were allowed to enter. Not only does this point out Judas's disregard for holy things, it also reveals his utter contempt for the priests to whom he betrayed Christ.

Whereas *hieron* is never used figuratively, *naos* is often used this way. *Naos*, the inner sanctuary, or inhabited place, is used five times in referring to Christ's body. All five of these references have to

35

do with Christ's statement: "Destroy this temple [*naos*], and in three days I will raise it up" (John 2:19). The Scriptures are clear, however, that Christ was referring to the "temple of his body" (v. 21). Christ's body was inhabited by God Himself, and therefore it was a temple in the truest sense of the word.

The word *naos* is also used when referring to Christians during the present age (I Cor. 3:16,17; 6:19, II Cor. 6:16). First Corinthians 6:19,20 contains the central thought: "What? know ye not that your body is the temple of the Holy Ghost which is in you, which ye have of God, and ye are not your own? For ye are bought with a price: therefore glorify God in your body, and in your spirit, which are God's."

Because the Holy Spirit indwells every Christian, the Christian's body is aptly referred to as the *naos*, or inner sanctuary. When we become fully conscious of this truth, it affects our associations (v. 16) and also our care of the body (vv. 16,17).

As we consider how the Jewish mind looked upon the temple at Jerusalem, it helps us to see how we should consider our own bodies. The Christian's body is the present-day Holy of Holies, for God Himself indwells it.

Chapter 8

'Form': Inner or Outer?

Much theological significance about the Person of Christ hinges on the proper distinction between two words in the Greek New Testament. These words are *morphe* and *schema*. *Morphe* appears three times in the New Testament (Mark 16:12; Phil. 2:6,7) and is translated "form" in each case. *Schema* occurs twice (I Cor. 7:31; Phil. 2:8) and is translated "fashion." It is interesting that three of the five uses of these words occur in three consecutive verses in Philippians 2 that describe the Person of Christ.

This chapter is perhaps one of the most doctrinally significant passages in the entire New Testament, and yet the Apostle Paul did not intend it for doctrine as such. Rather, he meant it to be an illustration of the humility of Christ so that the believers in Philippi could pattern their lives after Christ. In contrast to haughtiness and selfishness, the apostle said, "Let this mind be in you, which was also in Christ Jesus" (v. 5). Then Paul told what Christ did and thereby showed His attitude of mind. The crux of Paul's argument is that if Christ was willing to humble Himself, then Christians should also evidence humility in their lives.

Continuing with his thoughts about Jesus Christ, Paul said, "Who, being in the form of God, thought it not robbery to be equal with God" (v. 6). The word translated "form" in this verse is the word *morphe*. This word emphasizes a permanent, inner form that exists as long as the person exists. Since Christ is eternal, we know that He will always exist. Since He will always exist, He will always be in the "form of God." This verse proves that Christ has a divine nature; therefore, He is God.

Even though Christ, as to His very essence, is God, He "thought it not robbery to be equal with God." This phrase is difficult to understand as translated in the King James Version. A more literal, as well as more meaningful, translation is found in the New American Standard Bible: "Who, although he existed in the form of God, did not regard equality with God a thing to be grasped." Even though Christ was God Himself, He was willing to give up the outward manifestation of the attributes of God in order to come to earth to be the Saviour of the world. He did not give up being in the form of God, but He gave up His "equality" with God, as far as the manifestation of His attributes was concerned.

Philippians 2:7 sets forth the contrast: "But made himself of no reputation, and took upon him the form of a servant, and was made in the likeness of men." Here we have the miracle of miracles—Christ, whose nature is God, took upon Himself the nature of man, thereby becoming the God-Man.

Then we are told in Philippians 2:8, "And being found in fashion as a man, he humbled himself, and became obedient unto death, even the death of the cross." The word translated "fashion" in this verse is *schema*. This word emphasizes the outward appearance. As to His inner essence, Christ was the God-Man, but outwardly He appeared "as a man."

Some have departed from the teaching of the Scriptures to conclude that since His outward appearance was that of a man, then His inner essence or nature must also have been only that of a man. But the Scriptures make it clear that as to His *morphe*, or inner form, Christ was completely God and that at the Incarnation He became the God-Man. The Scriptures also clearly show that His humanity was entirely apart from the sin nature of man.

As we consider this passage of Scripture, we become overwhelmed with the thought that One who is God Himself gave up the privileges of manifesting His attributes so He could come to earth and take upon Himself the form of man to die on the cross for our sin.

Chapter 9

Subjection

There has been much discussion about the reference in Scripture stating that wives are to be in "subjection" to their husbands (I Pet. 3:1). Some have interpreted this verse to mean that wives are inferior in intellect and ability to their husbands. Others have used these words to show that husbands are to have complete control of every detail involving their wives. In order to gain a proper understanding of the verse, it is necessary to determine the true meaning of the word which is translated "subjection."

The Greek word that is translated "subjection" in I Peter 3:1 is *hupotasso*. The verse says, "Likewise, ye wives, be in subjection to your own husbands; that, if any obey not the word, they also may without the word be won by the conversation [behavior] of the wives." The word *hupotasso* is also translated "subjection" in verse 5: "For after this manner in the old time the holy women also, who trusted in God, adorned themselves, being in subjection unto their own husbands."

The word *hupotasso* is formed from two Greek words: *hupo*, meaning "under," and *tasso*, meaning "to arrange." *Hupotasso* thus refers to an arrangement of one thing under another. In relation to people, it refers to one person being under another.

In biblical times *hupotasso* was used most often as a military term, in the sense of "to rank under." A soldier who ranked under a superior officer would, in this sense, be in subjection to him. This did not necessarily mean that the lower-ranking soldier was inferior in his capabilities or capacities, but it did mean that as far as the line of authority was concerned, he was to be in subjection to his superior officer.

In checking other references where this same word is used, we see other fine shades of meaning. In Luke 10:17 we are told, "And the seventy returned again with joy, saying, Lord, even the devils are subject unto us through thy name." *Hupotasso* is translated "subject" in this verse. It is clear that the 70 had superior power and authority over the demons, because they were able to cast out the evil spirits.

The subject of I Corinthians 14:32 is the proper exercise of spiritual gifts. Paul was instructing the Corinthians regarding the proper limitations in using their gifts in meetings. For those who might say that they did not have any control over their gifts, Paul said, "And the spirits of the prophets are subject to the prophets." In this passage, *hupotasso* is also translated "subject." It is apparent here that Paul was telling the believers that Christians are to be in control of the use of their gifts.

In Luke 2 the word *hupotasso* emphasized the relationship Christ had with His earthly parents: "And he went down with them, and came to

Nazareth, and was subject unto them: but his mother kept all these sayings in her heart" (v. 51). In His earthly family relationship, Jesus ranked under His parents; therefore, He was subject to them. In addition to other things emphasized in *hupotasso*, the word suggests obedience in this passage. The same emphasis is found in I Peter 2:18, where servants are commanded to be subject to their masters.

In some verses, *hupotasso* is translated by the words "obedience" and "obedient." On instructing women about their parts in local church services, especially regarding the gift of speaking in tongues, the Apostle Paul wrote: "Let your women keep silence in the churches: for it is not permitted unto them to speak; but they are commanded to be under obedience, as also saith the law" (I Cor. 14:34). Here *hupotasso* is translated "obedience." In Titus 2:5 wives are commanded to be obedient to their husbands. Thus, *hupotasso* does emphasize the matter of obedience. This is clear in verse 9 of the same passage, where servants are exhorted to be obedient to their masters.

The word translated "subjection" in I Peter 3:1 involves power, authority, control and obedience. The husband ranks over his wife, not because he is superior in intellect or ability, but because God, in His divine order, has placed man in a higher rank of responsibility. This is evident in I Corinthians 11:3: "But I would have you know, that the head of every man is Christ; and the head of the woman is the man; and the head of Christ is God."

In I Peter 3:6 Sarah is singled out as an illustration of being in subjection to her husband. As one reads the Old Testament accounts about

Sarah and Abraham, it is obvious that Abraham required Sarah to do some things that were not especially desirable. But the Scriptures are clear that the one who was responsible before God was the husband. Because Abraham ranked over Sarah in responsibility, God held him responsible for her.

Many objections raised regarding this subjection commonly relate to situations where an unsaved husband requires his Christian wife to do things that violate her spiritual principles. We must remember that such a marriage is not the norm that God intends. The Scriptures are clear that believers should not be yoked with unbelievers (II Cor. 6:14). If both the husband and wife were Christians, perhaps 99 percent of the objections would be solved.

However, it is possible that both persons may have been unsaved at the time of marriage and that the wife became a Christian later. The question then arises as to what the wife should do. The purpose of I Peter 3 is to give the Christian wife instruction on how to win her husband to the Lord by being sweet and obedient. Because the husband will not obey the Word, he must be won by the tolerant reasonableness of his wife.

Paul commanded, "Husbands, love your wives, even as Christ also loved the church, and gave himself for it" (Eph. 5:25). When husbands obey this command, it becomes a joy for their wives to be in subjection to them.

Chapter 10

God's Wrath

The wrath of God is not a popular subject today. Theological liberals have explained away the truths of the Scriptures so that the popular belief today is that God is a God of love, not wrath. They teach that eventually everyone will be saved from condemnation, because God would not exercise wrath on anyone. The teaching of the Scriptures about the lake of fire is rejected because, they feel, it is unreasonable that there would be a place where men would suffer throughout eternity. Because God is a God of love, no one will suffer wrath from Him.

However, when one reads the Scriptures, he is brought face to face with verses that clearly refer to the wrath of God. The Book of the Revelation in particular emphasizes God's wrath. Before examining the verses which tell of God's wrath, it will be helpful to know the significance of the Greek words translated "wrath" in the New Testament.

Thumos is used 18 times in the New Testament. It is translated "fierceness" twice, "indignation" once, and "wrath" 15 times. This word emphasizes a turbulent commotion or boiling agitation of the feelings. It is often temporary, for it emphasizes an outburst of wrath.

Orge is used 36 times in the New Testament and is translated "anger" three times, "indignation" once, "vengeance" once, and "wrath" 31 times. *Orge* emphasizes an abiding or settled habit of mind, frequently with the purpose of revenge. In this regard, *orge* is more permanent than *thumos*. However, *thumos*—the boiling agitation of the feelings—can become *orge*—a settled or abiding condition of the mind.

Of the 18 times that *thumos* occurs in the New Testament, 10 are in the Book of the Revelation. Seven of the ten times in Revelation refer to the wrath of God. We are told that anyone who worships the beast and receives his mark will "drink of the wine of the wrath [*thumos*] of God" (14:10).

In the same chapter, the Apostle John tells of his vision of Armageddon: "And the angel thrust in his sickle into the earth, and gathered the vine of the earth, and cast it into the great winepress of the wrath [*thumos*] of God" (v. 19). Referring to the seven last plagues, or what is more commonly known as "the seven vials or bowls," the Apostle John says they are "filled up [with] the wrath [*thumos*] of God" (15:1). Verse 7 of this chapter emphasizes the same truth.

In chapter 16 the seven angels are instructed, "Go your ways, and pour out the vials of the wrath [*thumos*] of God upon the earth" (v. 1). When the seventh bowl of judgment is poured out, we are told, "And the great city was divided into three parts, and the cities of the nations fell: and great Babylon came in remembrance before God, to give unto her the cup of the wine of the fierceness [*thumos*] of his wrath [*orge*]" (16:19).

Referring to the fall of Babylon, Revelation 18:3 says, "All nations have drunk of the wine of the wrath [*thumos*] of her fornication, and the kings of the earth have committed fornication with her, and the merchants of the earth are waxed rich through the abundance of her delicacies."

When the Lord Jesus Christ returns to earth after the Tribulation, it is said of Him that "out of his mouth goeth a sharp sword, that with it he should smite the nations: and he shall rule them with a rod of iron: and he treadeth the winepress of the fierceness [*thumos*] and wrath [*orge*] of Almighty God" (19:15).

Thus we see that *thumos* occurs seven times in the Book of the Revelation in referring to the wrath of God. Five of these times it is translated "wrath" and twice it is translated "fierceness." Although *thumos* emphasizes an outburst of anger, it is obvious that this is only true from man's viewpoint. For centuries God has been holding back His wrath against sin, but during the Tribulation He will hold it back no longer and will pour it out on the earth.

Orge, which emphasizes a settled or abiding condition of mind, occurs six times in the Book of the Revelation, referring only to God's wrath. It occurs in 6:16,17, where we read of those during the Tribulation who say "to the mountains and rocks, Fall on us, and hide us from the face of him that sitteth on the throne, and from the wrath [*orge*] of the Lamb: for the great day of his wrath [*orge*] is come; and who shall be able to stand?"

When the seventh trumpet is sounded during the Tribulation, we are told that "the nations were angry, and thy wrath [*orge*] is come" (11:18). The preceding verse shows clearly that God is the Person referred to. *Orge* is translated "indignation" when describing the doom of the beast-worshipers during the Tribulation: "The same shall drink of the wine of the wrath [*thumos*] of God, which is poured out without mixture into the cup of his indignation [*orge*]; and he shall be tormented with fire and brimstone in the presence of the holy angels, and in the presence of the Lamb" (14:10).

As previously cited, Revelation 16:19 refers to God when it speaks of the "fierceness [*thumos*] of his wrath [*orge*]." Both of these words are also found in 19:15, which speaks of the "fierceness [*thumos*] and wrath [*orge*] of Almighty God."

Therefore, the Bible clearly indicates that God is a God of wrath as well as a God of love. He will exercise wrath on all who reject His Son as Saviour. All unbelievers will someday stand before the Great White Throne to be judged by God and then to be cast into the lake of fire (Rev. 20:11-15).

As seen from the use of *orge* in the Book of the Revelation, God has a settled wrath against sin. God has not only a permanent love for righteousness but also a permanent hatred for sin. The person who rejects Jesus Christ as Saviour will be eternally condemned, but whoever receives Christ as Saviour "hath everlasting life, and shall not come into condemnation; but is passed from death unto life" (John 5:24).

Chapter 11

The Great Commission

Evangelical Christians have no doubt about their commission to evangelize the world. However, there are differing opinions about just what is involved in "evangelism." Is a person evangelized when he has heard the gospel once? If so, all we have to do is make sure everyone gets a one-time hearing of the gospel and then our responsibility is fulfilled. However, it is obvious that many people who hear the gospel for the first time do not understand it at all. Our words are just so much noise if people do not understand what we are saying. Does this then mean that no person is evangelized until he understands the gospel? If so, much more is involved in evangelizing the world than making sure everyone hears the gospel once.

Before the Lord Jesus Christ ascended to heaven after His resurrection, He spoke these significant words to His disciples: "Go ye therefore, and teach all nations, baptizing them in the name of the Father, and of the Son, and of the Holy Ghost" (Matt. 28:19). On this occasion, when Christ commanded His disciples to "teach" all the nations, He used a word that is found only three other times in the New Testament. The word

48

translated "teach" in Matthew 28:19 is *matheteusate*. This is the verb form of the common word for "disciple." A disciple is a learner. He is a student, in contrast to a teacher.

The verb found in Matthew 28:19 also appears in 27:57: "When the even was come, there came a rich man of Arimathaea, named Joseph, who also himself was Jesus' disciple." The phrase "who also himself was Jesus' disciple" is literally, "who also himself was discipled by Jesus."

In Matthew 13:52 the same Greek word is translated "instructed" when Jesus said, "Therefore every scribe which is instructed unto the kingdom of heaven is like unto a man that is an householder, which bringeth forth out of his treasure things new and old." Thus again the teaching element of this word is emphasized.

This word is also found in Acts 14:21, which says, "And when they had preached the gospel to that city, and had taught many, they returned again to Lystra, and to Iconium, and Antioch." Here the word is translated "taught." Paul and Barnabas not only preached the gospel, they also discipled, or taught, many.

The preaching aspect of the Great Commission is seen in Mark 16:15: "And he said unto them, Go ye into all the world, and preach the gospel to every creature." But our responsibility is not fulfilled until we have also heeded the words of Christ recorded in Matthew 28:19: "Teach [disciple] all nations."

In Matthew 28:19 the words "go," "teach" and "baptizing" are all Greek participles. The

49

tenses of Greek participles are precise in pinpointing the time of their action in relation to the main verbal idea. The main verbal idea in Matthew 28:19 is the word "teach" [disciple]. Around this word all else revolves. The Greek tense of the word "go" indicates that the going takes place before the discipling. Obviously, in order to disciple the nations, we have to go to them by some means.

The word "baptizing" is in a Greek tense which indicates that the baptizing is to be done during the same time the discipling is taking place. As we are teaching others the Word of God, it is important that we be baptizing those who identify themselves with the Lord Jesus Christ. The idea is not that we disciple one year and baptize the converts the next; rather, the baptizing is to be done while the discipling is being done.

In addition to baptizing while discipling, verse 20 uses another Greek participle translated "teaching." This is the common word for "teach," and this verse precisely spells out what is to be taught: "Teaching them to observe all things whatsoever I have commanded you."

The responsibility of Christians is to disciple all the nations, thereby making them adherents to the teaching of the Word of God. Evangelism, therefore, is more than just giving a person a one-time hearing of the gospel. Evangelism, in essence, is teaching. It is teaching the unbeliever what God has said about his sin. It is teaching him what Jesus Christ accomplished on the cross when He paid the penalty of sin. It is teaching him how he can become a child of God by placing his faith in Jesus Christ as his Saviour. Having discipled a person in these truths, we can consider him evangelized when he is able to make a knowledgeable decision for or against Jesus Christ.

Chapter 12

A Saviour Is Born

The original language helps one to dig below the surface of the Christmas story in Luke 2 and gain many interesting insights. When you have discovered some of these gems, the reading of Luke 2 becomes an even richer experience.

Luke told us that Caesar Augustus gave a decree that "all the world should be taxed" (v. 1). The word translated "world" is *oikoumene*. This word was used originally by the Greeks to designate the land they possessed in contrast to the land of the Barbarians. When the Greeks later became subject to the Romans, the word was used in referring to the entire Roman world. Still later it was used to refer to the inhabited earth. It is from this word that we get the word "ecumenical." Obviously in Luke 2:1 it has reference to everyone under the jurisdiction of Caesar Augustus.

The King James Version indicates that the decree is for the world to be "taxed." The word translated "taxed" is *apographo* and actually means to "register" or "record." The decree was primarily that a census should be taken and people registered. Any taxation would be based on the census, of course.

Luke told us that Joseph and Mary went to Bethlehem so they could be registered. It was while they were at Bethlehem that Mary "brought forth her firstborn son, and wrapped him in swaddling clothes, and laid him in a manger; because there was no room for them in the inn" (v. 7).

The "swaddling clothes" in which Mary wrapped the Baby Jesus refers to swathing bands of cloth, which would be known in modern English simply as "cloth bands." There is insufficient support to maintain that these were rags, as some have claimed in emphasizing the poor conditions in which the Lord Jesus Christ was born.

Luke said, "There were in the same country shepherds abiding in the field, keeping watch over their flock by night" (v. 8). Historically, it is known that a flock was kept in the vicinity for the purpose of temple sacrifice. Although we cannot be sure that these shepherds were watching such a flock, it would be highly significant to the shepherds involved if the angel announced to them the birth of the Lamb of God, who came to be the sacrifice for sin and to put an end to the temple sacrifices.

The angel that appeared to the shepherds is not named, but his message was very precise. He told the shepherds, "Fear not: for, behold, I bring you good tidings of great joy, which shall be to all people" (v. 10). The shepherds "were sore afraid" (v. 9); literally, they "feared a great fear." When the angel spoke to them, he used a combination of words which emphasized "stop being afraid." The reason was that the angel bore "good tidings of great joy."

The word translated "good tidings" is *euaggelizomai*, from which we get our word "evangelize." It was good news that the angel proclaimed to the shepherds; therefore, they had no reason to fear. The angel said that the good news of great joy was to be to all people. In the Greek New Testament the definite article appears before "people," so the phrase should literally read, "all the people." The specific people in view was the nation of Israel, because Christ had come to be its Messiah and Saviour. It was then intended that the nation of Israel would proclaim the good news to all the world that Jesus Christ had come to die "for the sins of the whole world" (I John 2:2).

The angel emphasized to the shepherds that in the city of David was born a "Saviour, which is Christ the Lord" (Luke 2:11). The angel did not refer to the Lord Jesus Christ as "teacher" or "Great Example"—not even primarily as "Messiah," but as "Saviour." A saviour is one who brings deliverance, and Christ came to pay the penalty for man's sin so man could be delivered from condemnation by receiving Christ as Saviour. That He was also to be the Messiah of Israel is seen in His name "Christ," which means "Messiah."

The angel told the shepherds how they would recognize the Child: "Ye shall find the babe wrapped in swaddling clothes, lying in a manger" (v. 12). Luke recorded that after this announcement of the angel, "suddenly there was with the angel a multitude of the heavenly host praising God, and saying, Glory to God in the highest, and on earth peace, good will toward men" (vv. 13,14).

The phrase "on earth peace, good will toward men" is not the best translation of the Greek words. As translated in the King James Version, the phrase does not make clear the emphasis of the original language. More accurately, the Greek should be translated "peace among men of good will." This makes the meaning clear that only those who are well-pleasing (in right relationship) to God have peace. There is no peace for the person who has rejected God. The Bible emphasizes this when it says, "There is no peace, saith my God, to the wicked" (Isa. 57:21).

The shepherds went to find the newborn Saviour, and having found Him, they told others about the Child. Luke commented, "All they that heard it wondered at those things which were told them by the shepherds" (Luke 2:18). In contrast to these who were obviously discussing these matters publicly, Luke said, "But Mary kept all these things, and pondered them in her heart" (v. 19).

When Luke wrote that Mary "kept" all of these things, he used a word which intensified the normal meaning of the word "kept." He used a compound word which emphasized that Mary kept these things "with" or "within" herself. Luke also used a tense which emphasized that Mary continually kept all of these things in her heart.

Luke said Mary also "pondered" these things. The word translated "pondered" is *sumballo*, which emphasizes putting things together so one can consider or ponder them. Here we are given an insight into Mary's heart. While others were discussing the significance of the birth of Christ, as a mother she was inwardly reflecting about what she had been told and had experienced regarding the birth of Jesus. Mary obviously told her friends about many of these things, but as a mother there were some things that were too tender and precious to share with anyone.

Chapter 13

Praying Without Ceasing

One of the first things a new Christian usually hears is that all Christians should "pray without ceasing." Although he is slow to admit his problem to older Christians, the new Christian soon realizes that no matter how good a prayer life he has, by no stretch of the imagination could it be said that he prays without ceasing. He knows there are many times during the day when he is not praying; therefore, he feels guilty for not measuring up to the command of the Scriptures.

But what do the Scriptures really mean when they exhort the believer to "pray without ceasing"? The word that is translated "without ceasing" is *adialeiptos*. This adverb appears four times in the New Testament, and all references are associated with prayer. The first occurrence of this word is in Romans 1:9 where the Apostle Paul told the Roman Christians, "For God is my witness, whom I serve with my spirit in the gospel of his Son, that without ceasing I make mention of you always in my prayers." Here it is the making mention that is without ceasing.

The same Greek word appears in I Thessalonians 1:3, where Paul assured the Thessalonian

Christians, "Remembering without ceasing your work of faith, and labour of love, and patience of hope in our Lord Jesus Christ, in the sight of God and our Father." Here it is the remembering that is without ceasing, but verse 2 makes it clear that the remembering is closely associated with Paul's praying.

The third occurrence of *adialeiptos* is in I Thessalonians 2:13, where Paul wrote: "For this cause also thank we God without ceasing, because, when ye received the word of God which ye heard of us, ye received it not as the word of men, but as it is in truth, the word of God, which effectually worketh also in you that believe." Here it is the thanking that is without ceasing.

The last occurrence of *adialeiptos* is in the most commonly known reference, I Thessalonians 5:17, which records the Apostle Paul's command, "Pray without ceasing."

We see then that the adverb *adialeiptos* is used four times in the New Testament—and only by the Apostle Paul—and that all four references are associated with prayer. Paul mentions, remembers, thanks and prays "without ceasing."

The adjectival form of this word occurs twice and emphasizes the same meaning. One of these occurrences is in Romans 9:2, where Paul emphasizes the "continual" sorrow in his heart. The other is in II Timothy 1:3, where the word is again associated with praying. In this verse the Apostle Paul assured Timothy, "I thank God, whom I serve from my forefathers with pure conscience, that without ceasing I have rememberance of thee in my prayers night and day." Here the adjectival form of *adialeiptos* is translated "without ceasing," just as were the four uses of the adverb.

Thus we see that whether this Greek word appears as an adverb or as an adjective, five of the six times it is translated "without ceasing."

But the question remains: Is it really possible to pray without ceasing? The answer is found in discovering that during the Roman period, the word *adialeiptos* was used in describing a cough. No matter how serious a person's cough, it would not be one, long, drawn-out cough but rather, coughing at short intervals. Although at a given moment a person might not be coughing, it would not be said that he had stopped coughing.

The word *adialeiptos* comes from the word *dialeipo*, which means "stop" or "cease." The "a" prefix is the Greek way of making a negative, so that *adialeiptos* means "not stopping" or "not ceasing."

As we relate this information to the matter of praying, we see that the Christian is not expected to be involved in a single, never-ending prayer; rather, he is to pray constantly. ("Constant" implies uniform or persistent occurrence or recurrence.) Although we should always be in a prayerful attitude, it is obvious that we cannot be engaged in one continual prayer. Just as a person with a cough may cough frequently, we should be praying at frequent intervals for those whom God has laid on our hearts.

It should never be said of us that we have stopped praying. Instead, our goal should be to make the intervals shorter, so that less and less time elapses during which we are not communing with the Lord. Throughout each day we should be sharing with Him the things in our hearts. There should be a time each day when we have a concentrated period of prayer, but throughout the day we should be responding to the Lord and praying as we are led by the Holy Spirit.

Chapter 14

Dead or Alive?

Every spiritual blessing a believer has is the result of what the Lord Jesus Christ accomplished when He died on the cross. Many Christians are not aware of the centrality of the cross in providing not only deliverance from the penalty of sin but also deliverance from its power.

While some Christians have neglected emphasizing what Christ accomplished through His death on the cross, others have almost entirely concentrated their attention on the cross. As a result, many are still living at the cross, which is the place of death. It is important that we know what the Scriptures teach about the significance of Christ's death on the cross, but having seen those truths, we need to go on to further teaching.

The Scriptures emphasize two aspects of salvation. When a person receives Christ as Saviour, his sins are forgiven—but this in itself is not sufficient. If this were all that is accomplished by receiving Christ as Saviour, it would be like taking the bullet out of a dead man's head—the cause of death would be removed, but he still would not have life.

When we receive Christ as Saviour, not only are our sins forgiven but also God gives life to us. God imputes His righteousness to the one receiving Christ as Saviour. This truth is seen in II Corinthians 5:21: "For he [God] hath made him [Christ] to be sin for us, who knew no sin; that we might be made the righteousness of God in him."

There are two important things that happen to the person when he places his faith in Christ. One is that at that very moment he partakes of the benefits of all that Christ accomplished when He was crucified. Therefore, it can be said that the believer actually died with Christ. Romans 6 emphasizes the believer's death with Christ. But there is the additional matter of the believer's being made alive. We should understand and appreciate what was accomplished by our death with Christ, but we must not stop there. We must see the importance of living, which results from our being resurrected with Christ. Romans 6 also emphasizes this truth.

These fundamental truths are seen in the fine shades of meaning in the Greek tenses. Romans 6:11 is a key verse on this subject. In this verse the Apostle Paul wrote: "Likewise reckon ye also yourselves to be dead indeed unto sin, but alive unto God through Jesus Christ our Lord."

In the King James Version the adjectives "dead" and "alive" are used as if two states of existence are all that is being emphasized. Although this is not inaccurate, there is more that is emphasized in the Greek tenses. The word that is translated "dead" does emphasize an event which has already taken place. Each individual was potentially co-crucified with Christ on the cross. When he receives Christ as his Saviour, the believer receives the benefits of the cross so that his state of existence is that he is dead to sin. However, the word translated "alive" is not an adjective but rather a participle whose tense emphasizes continuous action in the present time. Thus, although the believer's death is referred to as a past event, he is to be living unto God. To say that a person is "alive" may mean that he is just existing. But to emphasize that he is to be living *unto God* indicates an abundant life that does not show up in the word "alive."

Galatians 2:20 brings out much the same truth as Romans 6:11. In the Galatians passage the Apostle Paul wrote: "I am crucified with Christ: nevertheless I live, yet not I, but Christ liveth in me: and the life which I now live in the flesh I live by the faith of the Son of God, who loved me, and gave himself for me." The word translated "crucified" is in the perfect tense in the Greek. This tense emphasizes that the act had been completed in the past and that its effect continues. The believer's crucifixion is a completed act of the past. It is not something that is presently going on.

However, in contrast to the crucifixion, which was completed in the past with a continuing effect, Paul said, "Nevertheless I live." The word translated "live" is in the present tense, as is the word translated "alive" in Romans 6:11. So also in Galatians 2:20 the Apostle Paul was emphasizing the living aspect of Christianity. He was not simply dwelling on what had taken place in the past; rather, he was emphasizing the abundant life which every Christian should be living. Paul became a partaker of the benefits of the crucifixion of Christ through faith, and his vibrant living for the Lord was also based on faith. Paul said, "The life which I now live in the flesh I live by the faith of the Son of God." The reason Paul had such an abundant life was that Christ was living in him and Paul was living by the faithfulness, or steadfastness, of Christ.

Not enough of us are "present-tense Christians." Most of us seem to be living in the past inasmuch as we are constantly looking back to what has been accomplished for us in the past. Our crucifixion with Christ is essential to life, but we must also emphasize the present tense of living for Him. We live for Him by making our lives available to His control so that He can effectively live out His life through us.

Sometimes one hears a Christian telling another that every day he is to crucify himself anew in order to properly live for Christ. Such teaching does not find support in the Scriptures because the Christian's crucifixion is something that has been completed in the past and will never be repeated. In supporting their crucifying-of-self teaching, many refer to Paul's statement in I Corinthians 15:31, where he said, "I die daily." However, the context does not bear out that Paul was talking about crucifying himself daily. In verse 30 Paul asked, "Why stand we in jeopardy every hour?" He was referring to the fact that he constantly lived in the presence of physical danger and possible death. This is supported by verse 32, where he said, "If after the manner of men I have fought with the beasts at Ephesus, what advantageth it me, if the dead rise not?" The

64

surrounding verses indicate that verse 31 refers to Paul's constantly living in the danger of physical death.

The Christian's need is not to crucify himself but rather to appropriate what Christ accomplished through His death on the cross. This is what Paul referred to in Romans 6:11, when he exhorted the Roman Christians to "reckon" themselves to be dead to sin but living unto God. They were to count as a fact their crucifixion with Christ and then go on to live for Him. We do not become spiritual by doing things for Christ; we become spiritual by appropriating what Christ has done for us.

Chapter 15
'Testing': for Good or Evil?

James wrote: "My brethren, count it all joy when ye fall into divers temptations" (1:2). In verse 12 of this same chapter, he wrote: "Blessed is the man that endureth temptation: for when he is tried, he shall receive the crown of life, which the Lord hath promised to them that love him." However, a problem arises when the next verse is read, because it says, "Let no man say when he is tempted, I am tempted of God: for God cannot be tempted with evil, neither tempteth he any man." On the one hand it seems that temptations are sent to us from God and we are to consider it a privilege to pass through them, but on the other hand we are told that God does not tempt any man.

In order to understand these verses, it is necessary to know the meaning of the words that are translated "temptation" and "tempt." The same Greek word is used in all three of the verses just quoted from James, yet there are obviously different shades of meaning intended. The word is used in its noun form in verses 2 and 12 and in its verb form in verse 13. The noun is *peirasmos* and the verb is *peirazo*. The root word of these forms has such meanings as "test," "try," "prove." The matter of significance about *peirazo* is that it is used in both a good sense and a bad sense. It can have the idea of testing with the purpose of bringing out that which is good, or it can have the idea of testing with the purpose of bringing out that which is bad.

When the word is used in regard to Satan, it has the bad sense of bringing out that which is evil or soliciting to evil. Satan himself is known as "the tempter" (Matt. 4:3). Satan thought he could get Christ to respond to evil, but because Christ is God, there was nothing in Him which answered to evil. Christ told Satan, "Thou shalt not tempt the Lord thy God" (4:7). Satan was not trying to bring out that which was good in God but was endeavoring to solicit Him to evil.

When Ananias and Sapphira lied about the amount they had received for their land, Peter asked Sapphira, "How is it that ye have agreed together to tempt the Spirit of the Lord?" (Acts 5:9). They were not trying to bring out that which was good in the Lord, so the word is used in its bad sense in this context.

The word *peirazo* is used in II Corinthians 13:5, where Paul told the Corinthians, "Examine yourselves, whether ye be in the faith." In this context the Corinthians were obviously to look at the good as well as the bad in their lives. So the word is also used in a good sense. Thus, in the Book of James, the "divers temptations" (various tests) have a good purpose in view—to bring out that which is good in the believers. This is why they should count it all joy. This is also true regarding James 1:12. However, the word is used in its negative sense in verse 13, as is evident from the

67

words "God cannot be tempted with evil." In the phrase "neither tempteth he any man," the words "with evil" are to be understood. Therefore, God never solicits a person to do evil but rather He brings tests into a person's life that will bring out that which is good in him.

First Corinthians 10:13 uses both *peirasmos* and *peirazo* in their good sense: "There hath no temptation taken you but such as is common to man: but God is faithful, who will not suffer you to be tempted above that ye are able; but will with the temptation also make a way to escape, that ye may be able to bear it." God sends tests and trials into our lives to bring out that which is good in us, and He always provides the strength necessary to bear up under the tests.

Another Greek word was frequently used when the writer wanted to emphasize a testing with the purpose of bringing out that which is good. This word is *dokimazo*. Whereas *peirazo* could be used in either a good or bad sense, *dokimazo* is used only in the good sense. In this regard it has to do with proving. In fact, of the 23 times *dokimazo* appears in the New Testament, it is translated "prove" 10 times.

One such occurrence is Romans 12:2: "And be not conformed to this world: but be ye transformed by the renewing of your mind, that ye may prove what is that good, and acceptable, and perfect, will of God."

Dokimazo is also translated "prove" in Luke 14:19: "And another said, I have bought five yoke of oxen, and I go to prove them: I pray thee have me excused." The excuse this person used for not attending the great supper was that he wanted to try out his yoke of oxen to see how good they were.

In I Corinthians 3, which tells of the Judgment Seat of Christ, *dokimazo* is translated "shall try" in verse 13: "Every man's work shall be made manifest: for the day shall declare it, because it shall be revealed by fire; and the fire shall try every man's work of what sort it is." This helps us to see that at the Judgment Seat of Christ the emphasis will be on discovering that which is good so it might be rewarded. Only those who have received Jesus Christ as Saviour will appear before the Judgment Seat of Christ. The purpose of the judgment will be, not to condemn, but to reward that which is good. The believer has been delivered from all condemnation through faith in Christ.

The understanding of this Greek word also helps us to see what God's purpose is in sending trials of our faith. First Peter 1:7 says, "That the trial of your faith, being much more precious than of gold that perisheth, though it be tried with fire, might be found unto praise and honour and glory at the appearing of Jesus Christ." The word "trial" is a noun form of *dokimazo*. Thus we see that the purpose for the trials of our faith is that God might bring out that which is good and that we might become mature Christians.

Because *peirazo* has both good and bad meanings, it can be used in regard to both God and Satan. However, *dokimazo* can never be used for Satan because he never tests to prove that which is good but rather to solicit to evil.

Chapter 16

A Decision or a Feeling?

What must a person do to come into a right relationship with Jesus Christ? When asked this question, a person acquainted with the Scriptures may quote such a verse as Luke 13:3, which records the words of Christ, who said, "I tell you, Nay: but, except ye repent, ye shall all likewise perish." A problem arises, however, in determining what all is included in the word "repent." The word is commonly used today as meaning only "to be sorry for." It is important to understand the true meaning of the word "repent," because those who do not repent will perish.

The word translated "repent" in Luke 13:3 is *metanoeo*. This word means much more than just being sorry for past actions; it emphasizes a change of mind.

When John the Baptist appeared in the wilderness of Judea, his message was, "Repent ye: for the kingdom of heaven is at hand" (Matt. 3:2). Because Jesus would soon appear as the Messiah, John wanted the people to be spiritually ready for His coming. John the Baptist was not asking the people just to be sorry for their sins; he wanted them to change their minds about Jesus Christ.

Those who did not realize their spiritual need for a right relationship with the Messiah obviously needed to change their minds about their spiritual condition and about the Person of the Messiah.

When Jesus Christ appeared, He was rejected as the Messiah and was crucified for claiming to be the Son of God. Because He was God in the flesh, man could not have crucified Him without His being willing. John 19:10,11 tells us, "Then saith Pilate unto him, Speakest thou not unto me? knowest thou not that I have power to crucify thee, and have power to release thee? Jesus answered, Thou couldest have no power at all against me, except it were given thee from above."

When Jesus died on the cross, His death satisfied God the Father for the sins of the world. The Apostle John wrote of Christ: "He is the propitiation [satisfaction] for our sins: and not for our's only, but also for the sins of the whole world" (I John 2:2). The question that remains is, How can Christ's payment for sin be applied to an individual? It is not applied just because a person is sorry for his sin. He may be sorry only because he has been caught in his sin, or he may be genuinely sorry because of the consequences of sinning. In either case, being sorry for his sin does not bring a person into right relationship with Jesus Christ.

What is needed in addition is made clear in John 1:11,12: "He came unto his own, and his own received him not. But as many as received him, to them gave he power to become the sons of God, even to them that believe on his name." It is necessary for a person to receive Jesus Christ as his Saviour in order to become a child of God. For a person to receive Christ as the One who has paid

71

the penalty for his sin, he must change his mind about his sin and about Christ as the Saviour. It takes an act of the will to receive Christ as Saviour. It is a choice which results from changing the mind about sin and about the Saviour. To those who make this decision, Christ Himself has promised, "He that heareth my word, and believeth on him that sent me, hath everlasting life, and shall not come into condemnation; but is passed from death unto life" (John 5:24).

Those who make the decision to receive Christ as Saviour doubtlessly have sorrow over the sins of the past and the wasted years of living for self. But it was not the sorrow that changed their eternal destiny; only the change of mind which resulted in the decision to receive Christ as Saviour was able to change their eternal destiny.

There is a word in the Greek New Testament which emphasizes sorrow and regret. This is *metamelomai*. This word is used in Matthew 27:3: "Then Judas, which had betrayed him, when he saw that he was condemned, repented himself, and brought again the thirty pieces of silver to the chief priests and elders." Judas sorrowed because He was condemned and even confessed his sin to the chief priests and elders: "I have sinned in that I have betrayed the innocent blood. And they said, What is that to us? see thou to that. And he cast down the pieces of silver in the temple, and departed, and went and hanged himself" (vv. 4,5). Judas was sorry because of his sin, but he did not have a change of mind about his sin and about Jesus Christ that resulted in his receiving Christ as Saviour. From the life of Judas it is evident that being sorry for sin is not enough.

If you have never made the decision to receive Christ as Saviour, remember from the experience of Judas that just being sorry for your sin will not enable you to escape eternal condemnation. Turn to Jesus Christ and receive Him as Saviour today. When you receive Him into your life, He will forgive you of your sin, deliver you from all condemnation, and give you eternal life.

Chapter 17

'Perfect': Sinless Perfection
or Maturity?

The word "perfect," as it appears in the King James Version, has caused some Bible students to draw the conclusion that it is possible for believers to live above all sin. Such a teaching is sometimes referred to as "sinless perfection." It teaches that believers are able to reach a point in life where they no longer commit sin. Some even talk of the old nature as being "eradicated," which enables the believer to live without ever sinning.

The word translated "perfect" is *teleios*. Its verb form is *teleioo*. The shades of meaning involved in these words reveal that something quite different from sinless perfection is intended by their use. In particular, these words emphasize that which is full-grown, or mature. Thus they often emphasize the finished product, whether it be maturity in a person or the finishing of a work.

The Apostle Paul wrote to the Corinthians: "Brethren, be not children in understanding: howbeit in malice be ye children, but in understanding be men" (I Cor. 14:20). The word translated "men" in this verse is the noun *teleios*.

74

It is evident in this verse that the Apostle Paul was drawing a contrast between children and adults. Paul was not encouraging the Corinthians to strive for sinless perfection but to evidence understanding that would be expected of mature adults.

A form of the same Greek word is found in Hebrews 5:14: "But strong meat belongeth to them that are of full age, even those who by reason of use have their senses exercised to discern both good and evil." Here the word is translated "of full age." Again it emphasizes maturity. This verse indicates that in order for us to become spiritually mature, we must exercise our senses in discerning both good and evil. We become mature as we make it a practice to apply the Word of God to daily situations.

James told his readers, "Knowing this, that the trying of your faith worketh patience" (James 1:3). Then he said, "But let patience have her perfect work, that ye may be perfect and entire, wanting nothing" (v. 4). Both of the words translated "perfect" in verse 4 are forms of *teleios*. James was emphasizing the end product of patience. The testing of faith works patience, which results in a mature, well-rounded Christian.

There will be a day when all Christians will be sinlessly perfect—when they leave this life and go to be with Christ. But concerning this life, the Apostle John wrote: "If we say that we have no sin, we deceive ourselves, and the truth is not in us. If we confess our sins, he is faithful and just to forgive us our sins, and to cleanse us from all unrighteousness. If we say that we have not sinned,

we make him a liar, and his word is not in us"
(I John 1:8-10).

The Christian today is to be "perfect" in the
sense that he is to be a mature individual who
honors the Lord in his daily living. Such a Christian
walks in accordance with the standards of his holy
God.

Chapter 18

Restoring a Spiritual Brother

The Apostle Paul exhorted all believers when he said, "Brethren, if a man be overtaken in a fault, ye which are spiritual, restore such an one in the spirit of meekness; considering thyself, lest thou also be tempted" (Gal. 6:1).

It is one thing to recognize the need of restoring a brother who has committed an act of sin, but it is quite another thing to rightly handle the situation. Most believers would want to avoid confronting such a person with his sin because of the reaction that might result. However, Paul presented the matter as an imperative for those who are "spiritual."

Those who qualify as spiritual Christians are those who live according to what Paul wrote in the previous chapter of Galatians. Paul instructed believers, "Walk in the Spirit, and ye shall not fulfil the lust of the flesh" (5:16). The characteristics of the spiritual person are known as "the fruit of the Spirit," listed in verses 22 and 23: "Love, joy, peace, longsuffering, gentleness, goodness, faith, meekness, temperance: against such there is no law." In verse 25 the apostle exhorted, "If we live in the Spirit, let us also walk in the Spirit." It is the

77

person who lives in accordance with these principles that Paul referred to as "spiritual."

Those who are spiritual are to "restore" the person overtaken in a fault. The word translated "restore" is *katartizo*. In order for us to know all that is involved in restoring a fallen believer, we need to know the shades of meaning involved in the word Paul used for "restore."

In tracing this word in its secular and biblical uses, one finds that it was used for reconciling factions. Certainly that is involved in Galatians 6:1. A brother needs to be reconciled. The word was also used in referring to the setting of bones. From such a use we can see that restoration often involves suffering. It would also indicate that the one doing the restoring must be knowledgeable about what he is doing. He would not want to cause unnecessary pain, but he would realize that proper treatment often involves pain.

In Mark 1:19, a form of this same Greek word is translated "mending" when it says that Christ "saw James the son of Zebedee, and John his brother, who also were in the ship mending their nets." Some commentators believe that the word refers to a "folding" of the nets rather than a "mending" of them, but in either case the nets were being prepared for further use. So also the spiritual believer is to restore a fallen brother so that he might be useful to the Lord.

When Paul used the word translated "restore," he put it in a tense which emphasizes continuous action. In choosing this tense, the Apostle Paul was stressing that such restoration involves a process, not just a single act. Those who have been used of the Lord to restore fallen brothers to a place of usefulness know the degree of patience and perseverance that is needed.

The Apostle Paul instructed that such restoration must be done "in the spirit of meekness." This is one of the characteristics Paul listed under the fruit of the Spirit, recorded in the previous chapter. While the word "meekness" is a rich study in itself, its chief characteristic seems to be that it combines strength and gentleness. The spiritual believer is one who is mature and strong in the things of the Lord and who has great compassion for those who are weak—those "overtaken in a fault." Meekness is the opposite of pride and is often used in contrast to pride. This is true even in the context in Galatians. In the last verse of chapter 5 Paul said, "Let us not be desirous of vain glory, provoking one another, envying one another." In contrast to being like this, Paul said that we should restore fallen brothers in the spirit of meekness.

Paul also reminded his readers, "Considering thyself, lest thou also be tempted" (6:1). When we realize that none of us are immune to temptations, it will cause us to be more gentle and sympathetic with others who have yielded to temptation. Every believer should realize that because he still has the old nature, he is capable of falling into sin. Such a realization greatly changes our attitude toward those who have fallen. In describing the attitude we should have, one Christian leader put it this way: "My brother fell today; I may fall tomorrow."

Chapter 19

Negative Commands

There are many negative commands given in the New Testament. When a person or group is commanded not to do something, the context usually indicates whether they were or were not doing it at the time the command was given. The Greek language had a way of indicating in its construction whether or not the action was going on at the time of the command.

If the action was *not* going on, the negative command would be given to forbid the action from ever beginning. To indicate this kind of prohibition, the aorist tense was used in the negative command. Such is the case in Luke 11:4, where Christ instructed His disciples to pray, "Lead us not into temptation." Because God tempts no man with evil (James 1:13), it is apparent in Luke 11:4 that the action had not been going on. It is as if the person praying were saying, "Don't even begin to lead us into temptation." The tense used in this negative command shows that the action had not been taking place.

When Jesus was crucified, the soldiers divided up His garments. But of His coat they said, "Let us not rend it, but cast lots for it" (John 19:24). It was not that they were rending, or tearing, it and decided to stop; rather, they had not begun to tear it. This is also evidenced by the aorist tense, which is used in this negative statement.

When the action *was* going on and a command was given for it to stop, the present tense was used in the negative command. When Jesus found the money changers in the temple and those who were selling oxen, sheep and doves, He drove them out of the temple and commanded them: "Make not my Father's house an house of merchandise" (John 2:16). The context makes it clear that they were making His Father's house a house of merchandise and that they were to stop doing so. Because the action was going on when the command was given, the present tense was used in the negative command.

With this in mind, it is interesting to notice Acts 18:9: "Then spake the Lord to Paul in the night by a vision, Be not afraid, but speak, and hold not thy peace." The question arises, Was the Lord telling Paul not to even begin being afraid or to stop being afraid? There are those who say Paul had no fear as he went everywhere preaching the gospel. However, the construction of Acts 18:9 uses the present tense in the negative command, thus indicating the Lord was telling Paul, "Stop being afraid."

It is true that the Apostle Paul was not ashamed of the gospel, for he wrote: "I am not ashamed of the gospel of Christ: for it is the power of God unto salvation to every one that believeth; to the Jew first, and also to the Greek" (Rom. 1:16). Although he had no reservations about the power of the gospel, this did not mean he was free of all fear in presenting the gospel. In I Corinthians 2:3, the apostle reminded the Corinthians, "I was with you in weaknesses, and in fear, and in much trembling." It is understandable that Paul would have had concern and fear as he came to the city of Corinth, which had a population of over half a million and which was full of perverted sex and wickedness of every kind. However, he had no reservations about the ability of the gospel to change lives if people would put it to the test.

Thus, in Acts 18:9 the Lord was commanding Paul to stop fearing and to speak. Verse 10 tells of the assurance the Lord gave Paul: "For I am with thee, and no man shall set on thee to hurt thee: for I have much people in this city."

In Romans 12:19 the Apostle Paul wrote the Roman believers: "Dearly beloved, avenge not yourselves." Here again the present tense is used in the negative command, indicating that they were avenging themselves and that Paul was commanding them to stop doing this. Paul then reminded the Roman Christians of the Lord's words: "Vengeance is mine; I will repay."

Chapter 20

A Condition or an Assumption?

In English the word "if" is commonly used to introduce a condition—"If you pay for this item, you may have it for your own." However, the word "if" is also used in the English language to indicate something that is assumed true—"If you are the owner of the house, you are responsible to keep it in good repair."

These uses of the word "if" were also common in New Testament Greek. Whereas in English we have to rely almost entirely on context to determine the use that is intended, the writers of the New Testament used different grammatical constructions to indicate what use of the word "if" they intended. By the different constructions in conditional sentences, the New Testament writers could indicate a condition that was assumed to be true, a contrary-to-fact condition, a more probable future condition, or a less probable condition. Perhaps the most unusual use to the English reader is that where the condition is assumed to be true.

In Mark 4:23, it is evident by both construction and context that the condition is assumed true: "If any man have ears to hear, let him hear." Because man does have ears to hear, he should hear and heed.

The Book of Colossians contains three verses where the word "if" does not introduce a condition to be met but rather something that Paul assumed true about the Colossians. Paul wrote: "And you, that were sometime alienated and enemies in your mind by wicked works, yet now hath he reconciled in the body of his flesh through death, to present you holy and unblameable and unreproveable in his sight: if ye continue in the faith grounded and settled, and be not moved away from the hope of the gospel, which ye have heard, and which was preached to every creature which is under heaven; whereof I Paul am made a minister" (1:21-23). The word "if" in the phrase "if ye continue in the faith grounded and settled" has the meaning of "since," or "because." Paul was not presenting a condition to be met; he was stating something true about the Colossians. Because the Colossians had been reconciled to God by their decision to receive Christ as Saviour, they could count on the fact that they would be presented holy, unblamable and unreprovable in His sight.

Concerning the Colossians, Paul also said, "Wherefore if ye be dead with Christ from the rudiments of the world, why, as though living in the world, are ye subject to ordinances" (2:20). Again the word "if" is used with the meaning "since," or "because." Paul knew that these people had received Jesus Christ as their Saviour and had died with Him, and in the light of that, he was asking why they continued living in subjection to human ordinances.

84

Paul also reminded the Colossian Christians, "If ye then be risen with Christ, seek those things which are above, where Christ sitteth on the right hand of God" (3:1). From the construction he used, we see that Paul was assuming that the Colossians had the right relationship with Christ, and because of this he was exhorting them to keep seeking those things which are above. Because of their position with Christ he urged them: "Set your affection on things above, not on things on the earth" (v. 2).

It is impossible to merit position with God. The way of salvation is the same for each person—by grace through faith. Even as salvation is not *ob*tained through works, neither is it *re*tained through works. Each person's salvation is completely dependent on the sufficiency of Christ's death when He paid the penalty for sins. However, having received eternal life through faith in Jesus Christ, there are a multitude of things the Christian can do to express this relationship to others. Good works are the result of a right relationship with Jesus Christ but never the means of attaining this relationship.

Chapter 21

Lackadaisical Following or
Intense Pursuit?

In giving inspired counsel to a young pastor by the name of Timothy, the Apostle Paul said, "Flee also youthful lusts: but follow righteousness, faith, charity [love], peace, with them that call on the Lord out of a pure heart" (II Tim. 2:22). Paul's counsel involved a twofold responsibility: fleeing and following. The Apostle Paul did not subscribe to the philosophy that a person becomes a stronger Christian by purposely submitting himself to temptation so that he might become stronger through resisting it. The clear command to Timothy was, "Flee also youthful lusts."

Paul knew that Timothy could not become spiritually mature just by avoiding certain things; therefore, he commanded him to follow that which was really important. Fleeing is the negative aspect; following is the positive.

The word the Apostle Paul used for "follow" left no doubt as to the efforts Timothy would have to put forth if he were to successfully follow these things. In commanding Timothy to follow, Paul used the word *dioko*. Of the 44 times this word appears in the Greek New Testament, 31 of its occurrences have to do with persecution. Christ used forms of this word in the Beatitudes when He said, "Blessed are they which are persecuted [*dioko*] for righteousness' sake: for their's is the kingdom of heaven. Blessed are ye, when men shall revile you, and persecute [*dioko*] you, and shall say all manner of evil against you falsely, for my sake. Rejoice, and be exceeding glad: for great is your reward in heaven: for so persecuted [*dioko*] they the prophets which were before you" (Matt. 5:10-12). At first it might seem strange that one word could have two such extreme meanings—that it could be used for persecution as well as for following that which is holy.

Paul used *dioko* in the sense of persecution when he said, "For ye have heard of my conversation in time past in the Jews' religion, how that beyond measure I persecuted [*dioko*] the church of God, and wasted it" (Gal. 1:13). The word *dioko* has the meaning of "to run after, pursue, strive for, seek after." Just as it is necessary to diligently pursue a person in order to persecute him, so Paul urged Timothy to diligently pursue righteousness, faith, love and peace. Paul was not referring to anything less than an intense pursuit— there is no lackadaisical following here.

Some Christians are frustrated because they do not experience all they think they should experience in the Christian life. Often this is because they settle down in the Christian life as if they were only going along for the ride rather than getting down to the business of pursuing that which is good.

We should make no mistake about the fact that Christ has fully paid sin's penalty and that we are completely delivered from condemnation by receiving Him as Saviour (John 5:24). Also, we need to realize that we are complete in Christ and that we are to appropriate what He has made available to us. However, let us not overlook the personal discipline which Paul exercised in following that which was good. He emphasized in his letter to the Christians at Philippi, "Not as though I had already attained, either were already perfect: but I follow [*dioko*] after, if that I may apprehend that for which also I am apprehended of Christ Jesus. Brethren, I count not myself to have apprehended: but this one thing I do, forgetting those things which are behind, and reaching forth unto those things which are before, I press [*dioko*] toward the mark for the prize of the high calling of God in Christ Jesus" (Phil. 3:12-14).

Although Paul realized his need was to appropriate what Christ had done for him, this never became a passive thing as far as his zeal in serving the Lord was concerned. Knowing that he was complete in Christ gave him a greater determination to expend every effort to know Christ and to make Him known. Because the truth of the grace of God had so captivated Paul's life, he could do nothing less than give an all-out effort to pursue that which was good for his own life and to do that which would make it possible for others to know Christ.

How diligent are we in our pursuit of the things of God? Are we content with a casual reading of the Scriptures, or is there a desire to dig deeper so that we might know more about Jesus Christ, who has done so much for us? When we attend church, do we let our minds drift from what is being said, or do we make a definite effort to concentrate on the things of God during that time?

When we appropriate more of what Christ has done for us in breaking sin's power over us, it will not result in passive understanding but in aggressive action to glorify Him.

Chapter 22

Is Lust Always Bad?

The word "lust" as it is commonly used today—though it has other meanings—usually refers to intense sexual desire. As you read the Bible, particularly the King James Version, you will frequently see the word "lust." This word is usually a translation of the noun *epithumia* and its verb *epithumeo*. It is true that these words were sometimes used in referring to intense sexual desire. Commenting on the commandment "Thou shalt not commit adultery" (Ex. 20:14), the Lord Jesus Christ said, "But I say unto you, That whosoever looketh on a woman to lust after her hath committed adultery with her already in his heart" (Matt. 5:28).

However, the words *epithumia* and *epithumeo* by themselves refer only to desire, usually strong desire. The context must determine whether it is a desire for good or a desire for evil. These words, referring to a desire for good, are both found in Luke 22:15, where Christ said to the apostles, "With desire [*epithumia*] I have desired [*epithumeo*] to eat this passover with you before I suffer." Thus, it is evident that these words can refer to a strong desire for that which is good. Of course, here the words are translated "desire" rather than "lust." But this fact in itself helps us see the true meaning of the Greek words.

The Apostle Paul also used these words in their good sense: "For I am in a straight betwixt two, having a desire [*epithumia*] to depart, and to be with Christ; which is far better" (Phil. 1:23). He also wrote: "But we, brethren, being taken from you for a short time in presence, not in heart, endeavoured the more abundantly to see your face with great desire [*epithumia*]" (I Thess. 2:17). The good sense of *epithumeo* was also used by Paul in referring to a church office: "This is a true saying, If a man desire the office of a bishop, he desireth [*epithumeo*] a good work" (I Tim. 3:1). The word "desire" in this verse is from another word which means to "aspire to" or "strive for."

Even when *epithumia* and *epithumeo* are used in the bad sense, they can have a far wider meaning than just intense sexual desire. In His parable of the sower, Christ said, "And these are they which are sown among thorns; such as hear the word, and the cares of this world, and the deceitfulness of riches, and the lusts [*epithumia*] of other things entering in, choke the word, and it becometh unfruitful" (Mark 4:18,19). These had a stronger desire for the things of the world than for the things of God.

In talking to the unbelievers in His day, the Lord Jesus Christ said, "Ye are of your father the devil, and the lusts [*epithumia*] of your father ye will do. He was a murderer from the beginning, and abode not in the truth, because there is no truth in him. When he speaketh a lie, he speaketh of his own: for he is a liar, and the father of it" (John

91

8:44). Unbelievers are in Satan's control and they serve his desires.

The desires of the old nature are referred to as the "lust of the flesh" (I John 2:16). The desires of the old nature are in direct conflict to the desires of the new nature in the believer. Paul wrote: "For the flesh lusteth [*epithumeo*] against the Spirit, and the Spirit against the flesh: and these are contrary the one to the other: so that ye cannot do the things that ye would" (Gal. 5:17). The strong desires of the flesh are against the Spirit, and the strong desires of the Spirit are against the flesh. The believer's formula for a victorious Christian life is given in the preceding verse: "Walk in the Spirit, and ye shall not fulfil the lust of the flesh."

Chapter 23

Paid in Full

In His Sermon on the Mount, the Lord Jesus Christ said, "Therefore when thou doest thine alms, do not sound a trumpet before thee, as hypocrites do in the synagogues and in the streets, that they may have glory of men. Verily I say unto you, They have their reward" (Matt. 6:2). In the last phrase, the word translated "have" is *apecho*. While the meaning is clear from the English translation, Christ's statement has even greater force when viewed in its original setting. The word *apecho* was used in secular Greek as a technical expression in drawing up a receipt. In this sense it meant "paid in full."

When used in the New Testament, *apecho* does not always have this technical meaning, but in several passages it is apparent that the technical meaning is intended. Such is the case in Matthew 6:2. Those who do their alms to be seen of men are paid in full by the praise they receive from men. When they are seen of men, it is as if they were handed a receipt marked "Paid in Full." They should never expect to receive further reward for what they have done.

The subject of verse 2 is the giving of alms. The word translated "alms" is *eleemosune*. It is from this Greek word that we get our term "eleemosynary," which refers to that which is related to, or supported by, charity.

Whether we are giving to the Lord's work or to a humanitarian organization supported by charity, if we give in order to be seen of men, we should consider that we have been paid in full for what we have done. We should not expect further reward from the Lord if our chief concern in giving was to be seen of men.

In verse 5 of this same chapter, the Lord spoke concerning prayer: "When thou prayest, thou shalt not be as the hypocrites are: for they love to pray standing in the synagogues and in the corners of the streets, that they may be seen of men. Verily I say unto you, They have their reward." The last sentence of this verse is exactly the same as the last phrase of verse 2 and has the same technical meaning of being "paid in full."

Public prayer usually presents a difficulty to every Christian. The believer realizes he is actually talking to God, and yet he feels he must be so conscious of his choice of words because others are listening. However, the New Testament encourages public prayer, and we should not avoid it because of our concern for what others may think. On the other hand, if we pray only because we are in public and want to be heard of men, then we have been "paid in full" and should expect no further reward.

Verse 16 of the same chapter comments on fasting: "Moreover when ye fast, be not, as the hypocrites, of a sad countenance: for they disfigure their faces, that they may appear unto men to fast. Verily I say unto you, They have their reward. Again the same phrase is used with the same meaning, but it is applied to a different subject.

Whether or not we should fast today is debatable. Men of God take their positions on both sides of the question. But at least in a general sense this verse can be applied to us who are living for the Lord today. Just as the hypocrites who fasted were concerned that they might be seen of men and have sympathy for their sacrifice, so present-day believers are sometimes guilty of wanting others to sympathize with them in what they have sacrificed. Some believers emphasize what a great position they could have had in the world as an unbeliever. Others tell of the pleasures of the world they have given up in order to live for Christ. Still others want people to know what a sacrifice it is to be a missionary or to be involved in full-time Christian work. Whenever we are guilty of so falsely playing on the sympathies of others, we need to realize that we have been "paid in full" by the sympathies and praises of men.

No Christian who knows the corruptness of the human heart would ever have fantasies about what he might have been apart from Jesus Christ. No Christian who has experienced the peace of God would ever be jealous of those who are "enjoying" the temporary pleasures of sin. No Christian who has grasped the meaning of the grace of God in his own life would ever call it "sacrifice" to spend his life telling others that Jesus Christ died for them also.

95

Because of what Jesus Christ has done for us, it should be our desire to please Him in everything we do. When this is the case, our reward will not all be received here on earth, but when we see Jesus Christ face to face we shall be "paid in full."

Chapter 24

'Appearance of Evil'

Have you known of some people who would not drink a soft drink from a bottle because alcoholic beverages also come in bottles and drinking the soft drink would have an "appearance of evil"? Or have you known of some who would not watch a Christian film, shown in a church, because non-Christians have used movies to show all kinds of perversion; thus, watching the Christian film would have "an appearance of evil"?

Those who have such views usually base them on I Thessalonians 5:22: "Abstain from all appearance of evil." This verse is commonly interpreted as reading: "Abstain from everything that might appear to be evil." The question that must be answered in properly interpreting the verse is whether the verse refers to doing things that are good but might appear to be evil or whether it refers to evil which appears in different forms.

The word translated "appearance" is *eidos*. This Greek word occurs five times in the New Testament: Luke 3:22; 9:29; John 5:37; II Corinthians 5:7; and I Thessalonians 5:22. It is closely associated with the word which means "to see," and thus *eidos* has to do with that which

97

strikes the eye or is seen. In secular Greek during New Testament times it commonly had to do with "form," because a form is something that can be seen. The word was found in the heading of a list of personal property and meant "list of effects." It was a listing or itemizing of that which was seen.

It is also interesting to note that the word "idol" was a compound Greek word, one part meaning "that which is seen" and the other part meaning "whole, entire." A person bowing down to an idol is giving himself to that which is wholly seen. But in a broader sense, whenever those living in the 20th century give themselves to that which is seen (materialism) instead of to that which is not seen (God and spiritual verities), they are idol worshipers just as much as those who bow down to idols.

Because the word *eidos* has to do with "form," a more accurate translation of I Thessalonians 5:22 would be, "Abstain from every form of evil." Romans 14 and I Corinthians 8 deal specifically with stronger Christians who do things which cause weaker Christians to stumble. It is true that the Christian needs to guard against doing anything which may not be evil in itself but which may appear to be evil and become a stumbling block to others. However, in I Thessalonians 5:21,22 the emphasis is on holding to that which is good and keeping away from that which is evil. Paul wrote that the Christians in Thessalonica should "prove all things."

The word translated "prove" is *dokimazo*, which means "put to the test" or "prove by testing." This word is used in I Peter 1:7, where it refers to gold that has been "tried" with fire. Just as in the testing of gold the impurities were to be removed and the gold kept, Paul was telling the Thessalonians to test everything and to hold to that which was good while abstaining from that which was evil—"every form of evil." Regardless of how spiritual a church or a ministry may be, evil can appear in many forms. The Christian's need is to be discerning so that he might abstain (keep away) from evil regardless of the form in which it appears.

Chapter 25

Kinds of Love

We commonly use the word "love" in many ways. We have one kind of love for our marriage partner, another kind for our children, another kind for our friends, and still another kind for various things in our lives.

In Greek, different words were used for "love" which showed the particular meaning intended. During New Testament times there were actually four words in use which emphasized different aspects of love. However, only two of these appear in the New Testament.

The word *eros*, which does not appear in the Greek New Testament, was predominantly used in referring to physical love. Eventually this word became associated with the lower side of love, especially in regard to passion. It is from this word that we get the word "erotic," which means "of, devoted to, or tending to arouse, sexual love or desire."

Another word in common use at that time was *storge*, which had mostly to do with affection within the family relationship. While it was used for the love a ruler might have for his people, it was mainly used in referring to the love of parents for their children and children for their parents.

This word is not used in the New Testament either, but words derived from it are. For instance, Romans 12:10 says, "Be kindly affectioned one to another with brotherly love; in honour preferring one another." The words "be kindly affectioned to" are translated from a word related to *storge*.

One of the ways of forming a negative in Greek is by prefixing a word with the letter "a." We have this in English in such words as "asocial," which means "inconsiderate of others" or "selfish." The negative of *storge* is *astorge*, and this word appears in II Timothy 3:3. In this verse Paul was describing some of the characteristics of the last days. He said it will be a time when people will be "without natural affection." The negative, *astorge*, is also translated "without natural affection" in Romans 1:31.

Another word which was commonly used in Bible times—and is frequently found in the Greek New Testament—is *philia*. This word especially emphasizes affection which grows out of mutual response. It is primarily an emotional love. This was the word that Mary and Martha used when they sent a message to the Lord telling Him about Lazarus. They said, "Lord, behold, he whom thou lovest is sick" (John 11:3). The word "love" in this verse is the verb form of *philia*.

The word that especially expresses God's love and the kind of love we as Christians should have is *agape*. This word has to do not only with the emotions but also with the will. It is the kind of love that loves even when there is no response. This is the word used for love in Romans 5:5,6: "And

101

hope maketh not ashamed; because the love of God is shed abroad in our hearts by the Holy Ghost which is given unto us. For when we were yet without strength, in due time Christ died for the ungodly." Although mankind was the enemy of Christ, He loved us even when there was no response, and He died on the cross for us.

It is this kind of love the Apostle John referred to when he said, "Beloved, let us love one another: for love is of God; and every one that loveth is born of God, and knoweth God. He that loveth not knoweth not God; for God is love" (I John 4:7,8).

The only way a person can have the kind of love that loves even when there is no response is to know Jesus Christ as Saviour. This is the kind of love He has, and when we receive Him as Saviour, He comes to live in our lives and works out this love in us. This kind of love is more than an emotion—it is a deliberate conviction of mind that determines a way of life. It involves an act of the will.

The Christian is not only to love those in his family, other Christians, and neighbors, but he is also to love his enemies. The Lord Jesus Christ Himself said, "But I say unto you which hear, Love your enemies, do good to them which hate you" (Luke 6:27). This kind of love results only from an act of the will, because certainly it is not an emotion where an enemy is concerned. It means that regardless of what the enemy does to us, we will seek only to bring about the highest good for him. We will be kind and will seek to win him to Christ, because we know this is his greatest need, even if he does not realize it.

Chapter 26

The Believer's Title Deed

Hebrews 11:1 says, "Now faith is the substance of things hoped for, the evidence of things not seen." Instead of the word "substance," some recent translations use the word "assurance." The Greek word that forms the basis for these translations is *hupostasis*. This is actually a compound word made up of the preposition *hupo*, meaning "under," and a word derived from *histemi*, which means to "stand." Hence, *hupostasis* refers to that which stands under anything.

This Greek word appears in only two books of the New Testament: II Corinthians (9:4; 11:17) and Hebrews (1:3; 3:14; 11:1). Assuming that Paul wrote the Book of Hebrews, this means that he was the only New Testament writer to use this word. In II Corinthians 9:4 it is translated "confident boasting," and in II Corinthians 11:17 it is translated "confidence" and is also associated with the idea of boasting. The element of confidence can be seen in this word inasmuch as it emphasizes a basis, or that which stands under. Because facts supported his boasts, what Paul said could be spoken of as "confidence of boasting."

In Hebrews 1:3 *hupostasis* is translated "person" and refers to the Lord Jesus Christ, "who being the brightness of his glory, and the express image of his person [*hupostasis*], and upholding all things by the word of his power, when he had by himself purged our sins, sat down on the right hand of the Majesty on high." *Hupostasis* emphasizes that which stands underneath, or substance; therefore, in the philosophical sense, it could have the meaning of "person," because it has the element of "substantial nature." In Hebrews 3:14 the word is used in its more normal sense of "confidence": "For we are made partakers of Christ, if we hold the beginning of our confidence [*hupostasis*] stedfast unto the end."

With these other uses as background, and with the knowledge that the word emphasizes that which stands under or supports something, a new dimension is added to our understanding of Hebrews 11:1: "Faith is the substance of things hoped for." In secular Greek of New Testament times, *hupostasis* was used in the sense of "agreement of sale." Thus it conveyed the idea of evidence of ownership. It would be valid, therefore, to translate Hebrews 11:1: "Now faith is the title deed of things hoped for." Faith is simply taking God at His word and acting accordingly. This kind of faith is the present title deed to what we will receive from God in the future.

The last phrase of Hebrews 11:1, "the evidence of things not seen," further expresses the thought of the first part of the verse. While the phrase, "things hoped for" refers to the future, the phrase "things not seen" can refer to past, present and future. The person who has taken God at His word concerning sin and the need to receive Christ as Saviour should have no difficulty in taking God at His word when He describes things that are not seen. The object of the believer's faith is God, as described in the Bible. Because this is so, there need be no lack of assurance concerning the things hoped for. We already have the title deed.

Chapter 27

The Believer's Help

The Apostle John used a Greek word in his writings that no other inspired writer of the Scriptures used. This word was *parakletos*. It is from this word that we get our term "Paraclete." In all, John used the word five times: four times in his Gospel and once in his first epistle.

The word *parakletos* is actually a combination of two Greek words. The first half of the word is the preposition *para*, which had the common meaning "alongside of." This Greek preposition is commonly found in the English language in such words as "paragraph" (to write alongside) and "parallel" (alongside one another). The other Greek word from which *parakletos* was formed was *kaleo*, which commonly meant "to call." From these separate words it is apparent that the compound Greek word *parakletos* referred to one called alongside.

In his Gospel, the Apostle John used the word four times (14:16,26; 15:26; 16:7). In each case the word refers to the Holy Spirit. In chapter 14, John was recording the words of Christ, who said, "And I will pray the Father, and he shall give you another Comforter [*parakletos*], that he may abide with you for ever" (v. 16). The disciples were concerned about Christ's statements that He was going to the Father, but Christ assured them that when He went to the Father, He would send them "another Comforter." The word "another" is *allos*, which means "another of the same kind"—the same kind as Christ had been to them. Thus the ministry of the Holy Spirit would aid the disciples in the same way Jesus had aided them while He was in their midst physically.

The ministry of the Holy Spirit as the Paraclete involves more than consoling. The word "comforter" falls short of conveying the full meaning, because we now think of the word as meaning only consoling. As a one-word translation of *parakletos*, the word "helper" conveys a more accurate meaning to 20th-century readers.

The Holy Spirit is One called alongside to help, and although this help includes consoling, it also includes many other things. This is evident from the other references in John's Gospel that refer to the Holy Spirit as the *parakletos*. Christ said, "But the Comforter [*parakletos*], which is the Holy Ghost [Holy Spirit], whom the Father will send in my name, he shall teach you all things, and bring all things to your remembrance, whatsoever I have said unto you" (14:26).

The Holy Spirit was to help the disciples by reminding them of the things Christ had spoken to them. This is also emphasized in 15:26: "But when the Comforter [*parakletos*] is come, whom I will send unto you from the Father, even the Spirit of truth, which proceedeth from the Father, he shall testify of me."

The 16th chapter of John's Gospel further delineates the ministry of the Holy Spirit. Christ said, "Nevertheless I tell you the truth; It is expedient for you that I go away: for if I go not away, the Comforter [*parakletos*] will not come unto you; but if I depart, I will send him unto you" (v. 7).

Christ then went on to say what the ministry of the Holy Spirit would be when He came: "And when he is come, he will reprove [convince] the world of sin, and of righteousness, and of judgment: of sin, because they believe not on me; of righteousness, because I go to my Father, and ye see me no more; of judgment, because the prince of this world is judged" (vv. 8-11).

It should be remembered that the Holy Spirit is not seeking to draw attention to Himself but is seeking to direct attention to the Lord Jesus Christ. This is evident from what Christ said: "I have yet many things to say unto you, but ye cannot bear them now. Howbeit when he, the Spirit of truth, is come, he will guide you into all truth: for he shall not speak of himself; but whatsoever he shall hear, that shall he speak: and he will shew you things to come. He shall glorify me: for he shall receive of mine, and shall shew it unto you. All things that the Father hath are mine: therefore said I, that he shall take of mine, and shall shew it unto you" (vv. 12-15). Therefore, the greatest evidence that the Holy Spirit has been able to accomplish His purpose in a person's life is that the person is completely taken up with the Lord Jesus Christ. It is important that we know how the Holy Spirit works so that we may be controlled by Him, but the Holy Spirit does not desire our attention to be upon Him but rather upon Jesus Christ.

The Apostle John used the word *parakletos* once in his first epistle, and there it clearly refers to the Lord Jesus Christ. John wrote to believers: "My little children, these things write I unto you, that ye sin not. And if any man sin, we have an advocate [*parakletos*] with the Father, Jesus Christ the righteous" (2:1). John went on to describe the Lord Jesus Christ by saying, "And he is the propitiation [satisfaction] for our sins: and not for our's only, but also for the sins of the whole world" (v. 2).

When Jesus Christ died on the cross for the sins of the world, He completely satisfied the righteous demands of God the Father. Therefore, having received Jesus Christ as Saviour, we have an advocate, or helper, who represents us before the Heavenly Father. How wonderful it is to realize that the grace of God is so marvelous that He has provided Jesus Christ as our advocate and intercessor in heaven and has given us the Holy Spirit to be our helper here on earth!

Chapter 28

Ransomed Forever

As the believer grows in his knowledge of the Scriptures and of Christ, he realizes he will never be able to fully understand redemption. But as he sees what his redemption cost God and what the results have been in his own life, his heart responds in worship to God.

There are three words in the Greek New Testament that are translated by a form of the word "redeem" in the King James Version. These three words are synonyms, so they have the same basic meaning; but they emphasize different aspects of that meaning.

The word *agorazo* appears 31 times in the Greek New Testament. It was used in the secular Greek of New Testament times to mean "to buy in the marketplace, to purchase." It comes from the word *agora*, which means "marketplace." Hence, *agorazo* had to do with buying or purchasing in the marketplace.

Of the 31 times *agorazo* appears in the Greek New Testament, it is translated by a form of the word "buy" 28 times and is translated "redeemed" 3 times. The three places where it is translated "redeemed" are all in the Book of the Revelation (5:9; 14:3,4).

In New Testament times, *agorazo* was also used in reference to the buying of slaves. The New Testament writers saw mankind as slaves to sin and used this word to show that Christ has bought us. The word is used in I Corinthians 6:20, where the apostle Paul wrote: "For ye are bought [*agorazo*] with a price: therefore glorify God in your body, and in your spirit, which are God's." Paul also wrote: "Ye are bought [*agorazo*] with a price; be not ye the servants of men" (7:23).

In order for anything to be bought, a price must be paid. Referring to the Tribulation saints, Revelation 5:9 tells of the price that had to be paid for them as well as for all believers: "And they sung a new song, saying, Thou art worthy to take the book, and to open the seals thereof: for thou wast slain, and hast redeemed [*agorazo*] us to God by thy blood out of every kindred, and tongue, and people, and nation." The redemption of man cost Jesus His life, for it was necessary for Him to shed His blood in order for mankind to be purchased from the slavery of sin.

Another word translated by a form of "redeem" in the King James Version is *exagorazo*. The "ex" prefix on *agorazo* is a preposition which emphasizes separation. Thus, this word emphasizes that which is bought *out of* the marketplace, whereas *agorazo* emphasizes the buying *at* the marketplace. In *agorazo* we see that Christ paid the price for our sin, and in *exagorazo* we see that He has taken us out of the marketplace of sin. He did not buy us to leave us under the domination of sin. *Exagorazo* appears four times in the

111

New Testament. Galatians 3:13 says, "Christ hath redeemed [*exagorazo*] us from the curse of the law, being made a curse for us: for it is written, Cursed is every one that hangeth on a tree." The word is also related to the law in Galatians 4:5, which tells us that Christ came "to redeem [*exagorazo*] them that were under the law, that we might receive the adoption of sons." Christ has taken us out of the marketplace of sin and out from under the dominion of the law.

Exagorazo is used twice concerning time. Ephesians 5:16 says, "Redeeming [*exagorazo*] the time, because the days are evil." Colossians 4:5 states a similar truth when it says, "Walk in wisdom toward them that are without, redeeming [*exagorazo*] the time." While it is possible in these two verses for the word to emphasize "buying up" the time, it seems that the emphasis is also "buying back" the time at the expense of personal watchfulness and self-denial.

The word *lutroo* appears three times in the Greek New Testament and is also translated by a form of the word "redeem" in the King James Version. The noun form of *lutroo* means "ransom," and *lutroo* means "to release on receipt of ransom" or "to deliver." In this word we see the emphasis on our release from slavery to sin because of the price Christ paid.

Lutroo occurs in Luke 24:21, which says, "But we trusted that it had been he which should have redeemed [*lutroo*] Israel: and beside all this, to day is the third day since these things were done." In this verse the emphasis is clearly on deliverance because of a price that was paid.

Deliverance is also seen in Titus 2:14, which says of Christ, "Who gave himself for us, that he might redeem [*lutroo*] us from all iniquity, and purify unto himself a peculiar people, zealous of good works." The third occurrence of *lutroo* is in I Peter 1:18: "Forasmuch as ye know that ye were not redeemed [*lutroo*] with corruptible things, as silver and gold, from your vain conversation received by tradition from your fathers."

How wonderful it is to realize that Christ not only paid the full price for our sin but that He also took us out from under the dominion of sin and set us free. Having received Him as Saviour, we are now free to please Him in all that we do.

Chapter 29

What Does It Mean to 'Yield'?

A key chapter on the victorious Christian life is Romans 6. From this chapter it is evident that the believer is to know certain things (vv. 6-10), is to reckon them to be so (vv. 11,12), and is to yield himself to God (v. 13). Concerning the matter of yielding, verse 13 says, "Neither yield ye your members as instruments of unrighteousness unto sin: but yield yourselves unto God, as those that are alive from the dead, and your members as instruments of righteousness unto God." Verse 16 further emphasizes the matter of yielding: "Know ye not, that to whom ye yield yourselves servants to obey, his servants ye are to whom ye obey; whether of sin unto death, or of obedience unto righteousness?" And verse 19 adds, "I speak after the manner of men because of the infirmity of your flesh: for as ye have yielded your members servants to uncleanness and to iniquity unto iniquity; even so now yield your members servants to righteousness unto holiness."

What all is involved in yielding to the Lord? Because the word "yield" in our common usage has a meaning of "surrender," it is often interpreted in only this passive sense when used in the Scriptures. But there is much more involved in the word.

Although technically there are two different Greek words used in Romans 6 that are translated by a form of the word "yield," both Greek words have the same basic idea, as one seems to be only a later development of the other. The older word, *paristemi*, literally means "to stand beside." Other related meanings would be "to place beside" and "to put at the disposal of." We are helped in our understanding of the word "yield" in Romans 6:13 when we realize it is the same word that is translated "present" in Romans 12:1: "I beseech you therefore, brethren, by the mercies of God, that ye present [*paristemi*] your bodies a living sacrifice, holy, acceptable unto God, which is your reasonable service." Thus, Romans 6:13 and 12:1 are emphasizing the same truth.

Paristemi was also used of servants, who "stood by" to do their masters' bidding. When Jesus was taken before the high priest after being betrayed by Judas, He answered the high priest in a way that displeased one of the officers who was listening. "And when he [Jesus] had thus spoken, one of the officers which stood by [*paristemi*] struck Jesus with the palm of his hand, saying, Answerest thou the high priest so?" (John 18:22). The officer who "stood by" was committed to carrying out the will of those who had authority over him. Such a person had not only yielded his will to serve the desires of others, but he was ready to aggressively carry out the will of his superiors.

The word *paristemi* is also used concerning the angel Gabriel. When he appeared to Zacharias, he said, "I am Gabriel, that stand [*paristemi*] in the

115

presence of God; and am sent to speak unto thee, and to shew thee these glad tidings" (Luke 1:19). Gabriel was at God's disposal and had been sent to Zacharias to announce that Zacharias and Elizabeth were to have a son.

Thus, when a believer yields to the Lord, it is more than just a "giving up" of his own plans and desires—it is a placing of himself at God's disposal to carry out God's will. It is true that only God can effectively accomplish a spiritual work, but He does it through believers.

When we make such statements as "I didn't do anything; I just let Christ do it all," we must be sure that our listeners know what we mean. Christ lives within every believer, as the Apostle Paul frequently emphasized, and Christ's desire is to live His life through the believer. We are to be yielded to Him in that we are to subject our wills to His, but we are to be active in that we are to carry out His will. We are to put ourselves at His disposal so that He can manifest His life through us and reach the world through us.

We have all that we need in Jesus Christ. Our responsibility now is to claim it and to go forward in aggressively carrying out His will.

Chapter 30

Hospitality

In the mad rush of our age it is difficult to find time to entertain friends. Evenings are usually loaded with meetings, but whenever there is a free evening, it is nice to spend it doing something with the family. Thus, it is obviously difficult to work in time to have friends over occasionally for a few hours of fellowship.

When we think of showing hospitality or of being hospitable, we usually have in mind the entertaining of our friends. Certainly this is included, but when the Bible talks about hospitality, it includes far more than entertaining friends.

The Apostle Paul reminded the Christians at Rome that they should be "given to hospitality" (Rom. 12:13). The Greek word translated "hospitality" is *philoxenia*. This word is made from two other Greek words. One of the words is *philos*, which means "friend" and is related to one of the Greek words for "love" (see ch. 25). The other word is *xenos*, which means "stranger." Thus the word *philoxenia* refers to a "love of strangers."

The hospitality to which the Apostle Paul referred included far more than having your friends over for the evening—it meant entertaining

117

strangers as guests. Nor did Paul see this as an easy thing to do, for the word translated "given to" is *dioko*, which means "to pursue" (see ch. 21). It takes planning and intense pursuit if we are to entertain strangers as we should.

Hebrews 13:2 shows the rewards of entertaining strangers: "Be not forgetful to entertain strangers: for thereby some have entertained angels unawares." A person who may be a stranger to us can be a messenger of God in that he brings something to our attention that we have not previously considered. Comments made by a stranger might well affect our entire lives as God uses those comments to give us a greater vision for His work and the world.

So important is the entertaining of strangers that the Apostle Paul gave it as one of the requirements for the office of bishop: "A bishop then must be blameless, the husband of one wife, vigilant, sober, of good behaviour, given to hospitality, apt to teach" (I Tim. 3:2). One who is to be an overseer in the church must, among other things, be a "stranger-lover." As Christians we will not have the impact that we should have on society unless we are really concerned about strangers; we must have a genuine love for people.

Paul emphasized this same requirement to Titus when he wrote: "For a bishop must be blameless, as the steward of God; not self-willed, not soon angry, not given to wine, no striker, not given to filthy lucre; but a lover of hospitality, a lover of good men, sober, just, holy, temperate" (Titus 1:7,8).

The Apostle Peter wrote: "Use hospitality one to another without grudging" (I Pet. 4:9). That

118

friends as well as strangers are included in hospitality is evident from the previous verse: "And above all things have fervent charity [love] among yourselves: for charity [love] shall cover the multitude of sins."

Christ said, "By this shall all men know that ye are my disciples, if ye have love one to another" (John 13:35). This includes showing our love not only to our friends but also to strangers. Are we "stranger-lovers," or do we love only those in our close circle of friends?

Chapter 31

Does God Punish Believers?

When referring to the fact of God's bringing adversity into a believer's life, the King James Version frequently uses the words "chastening" and "chastisement." On the other hand, some popular modern-language translations frequently use the words "punish" and "punishment" in the same verses. Three different but related Greek words are involved. The noun *paideia* occurs six times in the New Testament. The King James Version translates it "chastening" in Hebrews 12:5,7,11; "chastisement" in Hebrews 12:8; "instruction" in II Timothy 3:16; and "nurture" in Ephesians 6:4. Basically, *paideia* refers to "upbringing, training, instruction." The chief idea of this word seems to be that of discipline, and it is closely associated with training and education.

The verb *paideuo* occurs 13 times in the New Testament. The King James Version translates it "chasten" in I Corinthians 11:32, II Corinthians 6:9, Hebrews 12:6,7,10, Revelation 3:19; "chastise" in Luke 23:16,22; "instruct" in II Timothy 2:25; "taught" in Acts 22:3, Titus 2:12; "learn" in I Timothy 1:20; and "was learned" in Acts 7:22. As a verb, it has to do with the act of bringing up, instructing, training and educating. Like the noun *paideia*, the verb *paideuo* involves correction, because that is part of the process of training or educating.

The person who did the upbringing or training was referred to as a *paideutes*. This word occurs twice in the New Testament and is translated in the King James Version as "instructor" in Romans 2:20 and "which corrected" in Hebrews 12:9.

Altogether, these three Greek words—*paideia*, *paideuo* and *paideutes*—occur 21 times in the New Testament. Eight of the total occurrences are in Hebrews 12:5-11. This passage states:

"And ye have forgotten the exhortation which speaketh unto you as unto children, My son, despise not thou the chastening [*paideia*] of the Lord, nor faint when thou art rebuked of him: for whom the Lord loveth he chasteneth [*paideuo*], and scourgeth every son whom he receiveth. If ye endure chastening[*paideia*], God dealeth with you as with sons; for what son is he whom the father chasteneth [*paideuo*] not? But if ye be without chastisement [*paideia*], whereof all are partakers, then are ye bastards, and not sons. Furthermore we have had fathers of our flesh which corrected [*paideutes*] us, and we gave them reverence: shall we not much rather be in subjection unto the Father of spirits, and live? For they verily for a few days chastened [*paideuo*] us after their own pleasure; but he for our profit, that we might be partakers of his holiness. Now no chastening [*paideia*] for the present seemeth to be joyous, but grievous: nevertheless afterward it yieldeth the peaceable fruit of righteousness unto them which are exercised thereby."

Another word for "chastise" is "discipline." This would perhaps be a better translation of these Greek words than either "chastise" or "punish." To some extent "chastise" and "punish" are interchangeable, yet each seems to have its own emphasis. "Punish" is more negative in that it involves correction for wrongdoing. "Chastise," or "discipline," is more positive in that its purpose is to motivate to better behavior. Certainly "discipline" would include a penalty for wrongdoing, but it has a teaching purpose—it is not an end in itself.

In his book *Reality Therapy*, psychiatrist William Glasser distinguishes between discipline and punishment. In the chapter entitled "The Treatment of Seriously Delinquent Adolescent Girls" Dr. Glasser writes: "Girls are willing to accept discipline but not punishment; they differentiate between the two by seeing whether the disciplining person shows anger and gets satisfaction by exercising power" (p. 78).

God does not chastise believers because He receives satisfaction from it or wants to display His power; He chastises us because He wants to accomplish something in our lives that will be for our good and His glory. God disciplines and allows adversity into our lives because He knows "that the trial of [our] faith is more precious than of gold that perisheth" and that it is through the trial of our faith that we will be "found unto praise and honour and glory at the appearing of Jesus Christ" (I Pet. 1:7).

Closely associated with the fact that "all things work together for [the] good" of believers is the fact that God has predestinated believers to "be

122

conformed to the image of his Son" (Rom. 8:28,29). The purpose of God's discipline is to conform us to the image of Jesus Christ.

Above all, we should realize that God does not punish believers in the sense of condemning. Jesus Christ has taken all our condemnation upon Himself. The Lord Jesus assured believers, "He that heareth my word, and believeth on him that sent me, hath everlasting life, and shall not come into condemnation; but is passed from death unto life" (John 5:24).

We are not serving an angry God who loves to punish us every time we fail; rather we are serving a God of grace who has borne all our condemnation and who now wants to live His life through us. True, He corrects us for wrongdoing, but His purpose is to bring about more responsible behavior from us which will be glorifying to Him.

Chapter 32

Needed: More Examples, More Mimics

We get our word "type" from the word *tupos*, which occurs 16 times in the Greek New Testament. At first, the word was used to refer to a strike, or blow, and came to emphasize the mark or impression left by a blow. The word also had the idea of "pattern," for the mark left was a pattern of that which delivered the blow. Just as an official seal, such as that used by a corporation or an educational institution, leaves its pattern or impression, the person who is a *tupos* leaves his impression on others, so that they reflect him.

It is in this sense that a believer is to be a model, or pattern, for other believers. Paul told the Philippian believers, "Ye have us for an ensample [*tupos*]" (Phil. 3:17). The Philippian believers were to pattern their lives after Paul and other mature believers. In fact, Paul sometimes did things specifically for the purpose of being an example. When he was in Thessalonica, he purposely earned his own living in order to set an example for believers. Reminding them later of this fact, Paul said, "Neither did we eat any man's bread for nought; but wrought with labour and travail night and day, that we might not be chargeable to any of you: not because we have not power [authority], but to make ourselves an ensample [*tupos*] unto you to follow us" (II Thess. 3:8,9). The Apostle Peter exhorted those in positions of spiritual leadership, "Feed the flock of God which is among you, taking the oversight thereof, not by constraint, but willingly; not for filthy lucre, but of a ready mind; neither as being lords over God's heritage, but being ensamples [*tupos*] to the flock" (I Pet. 5:2,3). Just as we reap what we sow, those to whom we minister will reflect us. It is important, therefore, that we be good examples for them to follow.

The Scriptures also emphasize the importance of *following* good examples. The Apostle Paul wrote to the Corinthian believers: "Wherefore I beseech you, be ye followers of me" (I Cor. 4:16). The word translated "followers" is *mimetes*, from which we get our word "mimic."

Although the word "mimic" is often thought of in a bad sense, in the New Testament this Greek word was always used in a good sense. Thus, Paul was exhorting the Corinthians to mimic his way of life. Paul made it clear, however, why it was safe to make such an exhortation—it was because he was mimicking Jesus Christ. Paul said, "Be ye followers [*mimetes*] of me, even as I also am of Christ" (I Cor. 11:1). When we make it our chief goal to imitate Jesus Christ in our daily living, it will be safe for us to urge others to imitate us. Paul was not saying that he never made mistakes, but he was encouraging others to make Christ central in their thinking, even as he had in his.

Paul reminded the believers in Thessalonica, "And ye became followers [*mimetes*] of us, and of the Lord, having received the word in much affliction, with joy of the Holy Ghost: so that ye were ensamples [*tupos*] to all that believe in Macedonia and Achaia" (I Thess. 1:6,7). Because the believers in Thessalonica had imitated, or mimicked, the Lord and also mature believers, they became models for others. Thus we see that one must pattern his life after the Lord before he can become a good pattern for others to follow.

Our need, then, is to saturate our lives with the Word of God so that we might know how to properly imitate the Lord in any situation. At the same time, we will become good examples for others to follow.

Chapter 33

Building Spiritual Houses

One frequently hears the expression "building up Christians in the faith." This is a scriptural expression, because it is based on many New Testament verses, especially those written by the Apostle Paul.

In New Testament times, the common word for "building," or "building up," was *oikodomeo*. This verb was formed by joining *oikos*, meaning "house," and *demo*, meaning "to build." Thus, the word *oikodomeo* literally meant "to build a house," but it was applied to building in general.

The Apostle Paul chose this common word for "building" and applied it to Christians. In I Corinthians he used both the noun *oikodome*, meaning "building," and the verb *oikodomeo*, meaning "to build."

Paul told the Corinthian believers, "Ye are God's building [*oikodome*]" (3:9). Concerning what he had done for the Corinthians, Paul said, "As a wise masterbuilder, I have laid the foundation, and another buildeth thereon. But let every man take heed how he buildeth thereupon. For other foundation can no man lay than that is laid, which is Jesus Christ" (vv. 10,11). Paul had told the Corinthians about Jesus Christ, and those who responded by receiving Him as Saviour were said to have had the foundation laid in their lives. Everything else of spiritual value had to be laid on that foundation, Jesus Christ.

Paul then referred to those who would be building on the lives of the Corinthian believers when he said, "Now if any man build [*oikodomeo*] upon this foundation gold, silver, precious stones, wood, hay, stubble; every man's work shall be made manifest: for the day shall declare it, because it shall be revealed by fire; and the fire shall try every man's work of what sort it is" (vv. 12,13).

This passage of Scripture is commonly explained as teaching that the person who stands before the Lord will be rewarded for the good in his life. But Paul seems to be emphasizing that when one believer stands before the Lord to have his life evaluated, others will be rewarded according to the way they built on that believer's life. Other passages of Scripture indicate that believers will stand before the Lord and be rewarded for what they have done for Him (II Cor. 5:10), but the emphasis in I Corinthians 3 is placed on the building process of what one person has done in another person's life. When the building is evaluated, the builder will be rewarded according to the quality of work he has built on the foundation, Jesus Christ.

One of Paul's major reasons for writing I Corinthians was to get the Corinthian believers to be more concerned about other believers. Therefore, he emphasized building on the foundation in others' lives.

The Corinthian believers were carnal; that is, they were more concerned about pleasing themselves than about pleasing Christ (3:1-4). They insisted on having their own rights rather than being concerned for others.

Selfishness was the main problem in the case Paul dealt with in chapter 8. Older believers insisted on doing what they knew was technically right, even though they were being stumbling blocks to weaker Christians. Paul reminded the Corinthian believers, "Knowledge puffeth up, but charity [love] edifieth [*oikodomeo*]" (v. 1). In this verse we have one of the common ways the King James Version's translators rendered *oikodomeo*. When referring to building up another person, they frequently translated the Greek word by a form of the word "edify."

Paul warned the Corinthian believers that by demanding their own rights, they were doing the wrong kind of building in the lives of weaker Christians. He told them, "For if any man see thee which hast knowledge sit at meat in the idol's temple, shall not the conscience of him which is weak be emboldened [*oikodomeo*] to eat those things which are offered to idols" (v. 10). Certainly, a believer who builds in the wrong way in another person's life will not receive a reward for what he has done. Unwise actions by older believers can cause spiritual shipwreck to young believers. When we are motivated by love, we will not want to cause another person to stumble in his Christian walk. Paul emphasized the seriousness of causing others to stumble when he said, "But when ye sin so against the brethren, and wound their weak conscience, ye sin against Christ" (v. 12).

Touching on the Christian's liberty in things not specifically prohibited by God's Word, Paul said, "All things are lawful for me, but all things are not expedient: all things are lawful for me, but all things edify [*oikodomeo*] not" (10:23). In the realm of Christian liberty, our concern should be to do that which encourages other Christians in the faith. When we insist on our own rights and flaunt our liberty, we are not manifesting the fruit of the indwelling Holy Spirit.

Other occurrences of *oikodomeo* and *oikodome* are found in I Corinthians 14, where Paul dealt with the specific problem of speaking in tongues. Here again, the Corinthian believers were not considerate of the needs of other believers. They were far more concerned about exercising the gifts of the Spirit than they were about demonstrating the fruit of the Spirit. Paul told them, "He that prophesieth speaketh unto men to edification [*oikodome*] and exhortation, and comfort. He that speaketh in an unknown tongue edifieth [*oikodomeo*] himself; but he that prophesieth edifieth [*oikodomeo*] the church" (vv. 3,4).

It does not seem that Paul was commending the believers for edifying themselves by speaking in tongues; rather, he was reprimanding them for not being concerned about edifying the Church, or other believers. Paul went on to tell them, "I would that ye all spake with tongues, but rather that ye prophesied: for greater is he that prophesieth than he that speaketh with tongues, except he interpret, that the church may receive edifying [*oikodome*]" (v. 5).

130

Paul emphasized a concern for others when he wrote: "Even so ye, forasmuch as ye are zealous of spiritual gifts, seek that ye may excel to the edifying [*oikodome*] of the church" (v. 12). The major concern when believers assemble is that everything which is done should result in encouraging and building up one another in the faith. For believers to be edified, they must understand what is being said. To those so concerned about speaking in tongues even when others could not understand, Paul said, "For thou verily givest thanks well, but the other is not edified [*oikodomeo*]" (v. 17).

The key phrase of I Corinthians 14 may well be Paul's statement in verse 26: "Let all things be done unto edifying [*oikodome*]."

Chapter 34

What Kind of Fear Is From God?

The seasoned Apostle Paul told young Timothy, "God hath not given us the spirit of fear; but of power, and of love, and of a sound mind" (II Tim. 1:7).

This verse is difficult to understand when one remembers what the Scriptures say about fear. Proverbs 9:10 says, "The fear of the Lord is the beginning of wisdom: and the knowledge of the holy is understanding." Exodus 23:27 says, "I will send my fear before thee, and will destroy all the people to whom thou shalt come, and I will make all thine enemies turn their backs unto thee."

With verses such as these, which clearly indicate that fear can have its origin in God, how does one explain II Timothy 1:7: "God hath not given us the spirit of fear"? The answer is found in an understanding of the Greek word that is translated "fear."

When Paul assured Timothy that the attitude of fear did not originate with God, he used the word *deilia*. In this exact form, this is the only time *deilia* occurs in the New Testament. However, other closely related words appear in the Greek New Testament. The related words are *deiliao*

(John 14:27) and *deilos* (Matt. 8:26; Mark 4:40; Rev. 21:8).

Deiliao is translated "let it be afraid" in John 14:27, which records the words of Jesus: "Peace I leave with you, my peace I give unto you: not as the world giveth, give I unto you. Let not your heart be troubled, neither let it be afraid." The Lord didn't want His followers to be cowards as they contemplated what it would be like without Him on earth. They had no need to be cowardly, because He promised to be with them always, even though He would be physically absent.

Deilos is translated "fearful" in all three of its occurrences in the New Testament. Matthew 8:26 says, "And he saith unto them, Why are ye fearful [*deilos*] O ye of little faith? Then he arose, and rebuked the winds and the sea; and there was a great calm." Mark 4:40 also uses this word: "Why are ye so fearful [*deilos*]? how is it that ye have no faith?" Revelation 21:8 tells of the final destiny of those who reject Jesus Christ as Saviour: "But the fearful [*deilos*], and unbelieving, and the abominable, and murderers, and whoremongers, and sorcerers, and idolaters, and all liars, shall have their part in the lake which burneth with fire and brimstone: which is the second death."

None of these Greek words are used in a positive way in the New Testament. All of them denote the sense of cowardice. Therefore, Paul was able to assure Timothy that this kind of fear does not come from the Lord. It is one thing to be afraid when there is a justifiable cause, but it is quite another thing to let fear control one's entire life. This is cowardice and does not originate with God.

Some recent translations use "timidity" to render the word *deilia* in II Timothy 1:7. Our English word "timid" is derived from a Latin word which means "to fear." If one is aware of the element of fear in the words "timid" and "timidity," then he can understand why "timidity" is a good translation of *deilia* in this verse.

Above all, the Christian should not be afraid of new circumstances, for he serves the "Christ of every crisis." Certainly the child of God will not be without fear when there is reason to fear; but he will not let fear dominate his life. His confidence will be in God.

The Old Testament experiences of the Israelites were written "for our admonition" (I Cor. 10:11). One of the key experiences of these people was at Kadesh-barnea, where they sent 12 spies into Canaan to see what the land was like. When the spies returned, ten of them gave a negative report on the Israelites' chances of gaining control of the land. These spies said, "We be not able to go up against the people; for they are stronger than we" (Num. 13:31). Because these spies were concentrating more on the circumstances than on God, they didn't think there was any possibility that the Israelites could take the land.

The other two spies, Joshua and Caleb, trusted God and His ability to fulfill His promises. They concentrated more on God than on the circumstances, and Caleb spoke for both of them when he said, "Let us go up at once, and possess it; for we are well able to overcome it" (v. 30).

134

The attitude of the ten spies did not originate with God, because it was one of cowardice. They refused to believe God.

Often the reason for our reluctance about doing God's will is that we think more about circumstances than about God. When this happens, we yield to the same unbelief and cowardice as did the ten spies. This fear does not come from God.

Chapter 35

Peace—God's Umpire

One of the most significant of the verses that tell Christians how to know the will of God is Colossians 3:15. On the surface, the verse does not seem so crucial to the subject, because its force does not come through in many English translations. The King James Version translates this verse, "Let the peace of God rule in your hearts, to the which also ye are called in one body; and be ye thankful."

The Greek word that is translated "rule" is *brabeuo*. Colossians 3:15 is the only place where this word occurs in the Greek New Testament. The word "rule" is an acceptable translation of *brabeuo* as long as one understands its complete meaning.

During New Testament times *brabeuo* was used in secular literature when describing court proceedings and athletic contests. The word emphasized a decision, such as one made by the court or by an umpire. *Brabeuo* means "to arbitrate, decide, to act as an umpire." With this in mind, it is easy to see how "rule" is an acceptable translation of the Greek word. The decision of the court and the decision of the umpires would rule in their respective areas of authority.

Applying the significance of this word to Colossians 3:15, we understand better how the Lord's will can be determined. We are to let the peace of God "act as umpire" in our hearts. Whenever we have an inner dispute about what we should do, God's peace should be the arbitrator.

God never directs His children to do something that is contrary to His written Word. Therefore, Christians should diligently study the Bible to know if a certain thing is wrong according to the Scriptures. However, sometimes the most difficult matter in the Christian life is not choosing between things that are definitely right or definitely wrong. When confronted with this decision the Christian should do what is right. The greatest difficulty he usually faces is deciding between two or more things that are right—determining what is best in contrast to what is good.

After he has carefully studied the portions of God's Word that deal with his problem, the Christian may be sure that none of the options he faces are wrong in God's sight, yet he can do only one thing. In this situation the peace of God helps him to decide what is best. He must allow the peace of God to call the decision. His whole life should be ruled by this peace, and he should make no decisions that disturb God's peace within him.

As the child of God prays concerning his open options, he will discover that the peace of God will indicate which alternative to follow. This is assuming, of course, that he wants to please Jesus Christ in everything. When this is the Christian's motive, he can be sure that the indwelling Holy Spirit will tell him, by giving him the peace of God, what decision to make.

137

One may not be able to explain this peace to others or even adequately defend his decision, but he can be convinced that he has chosen God's will. That this peace is inexplainable is emphasized in Philippians 4:6,7: "Be careful for nothing; but in every thing by prayer and supplication with thanksgiving let your requests be made known unto God. And the peace of God, which passeth all understanding, shall keep your hearts and minds through Christ Jesus." Often the Christian cannot understand or explain God's peace, because God is infinite and man is finite. The marvel of it all is not only that the infinite God has given man a revelation of Himself through the Bible but also that He communicates to man by means of peace.

Christians need to be sensitive to sin and to present themselves unreservedly to do God's will. When this is the case, the Spirit of God will use the Word of God to produce the peace of God in their lives.

Chapter 36

Persistence Isn't Enough

The Greek word *akribos* and its other forms are often translated "diligent" or "diligently." The English word "diligent" is commonly used to mean "persistent." One who does not give up but continues to work on a task is a "diligent" person.

Though *akribos* includes the idea of diligence, there is an even finer shade of meaning to this word and its other forms—the basic meaning is that of accuracy, or exactness. It is an accuracy which is the outcome of carefulness.

When the Wise Men came from the east to Jerusalem, looking for the One who was born King of the Jews, Herod called them aside privately and "enquired of them diligently [*akribos*] what time the star appeared" (Matt. 2:7). Herod was careful to find out exactly when these men first saw the star in the east. After questioning the Wise Men, Herod "sent them to Bethlehem, and said, Go and search diligently [*akribos*] for the young child" (v. 8). Herod was concerned not only that the Wise Men should persistently search for the young Child but also that they should search accurately, or exactly, to make sure that He was the precise Child they were looking for. Herod was already plotting

139

to destroy this rival King, and he wanted to be sure to eliminate the right Person.

When the Wise Men did not return to Herod with their report, he became exceedingly angry and "sent forth, and slew all the children that were in Bethlehem, and in all the coasts thereof, from two years old and under, according to the time which he had diligently [*akribos*] enquired of the wise men" (v. 16). This verse refers to Herod's careful questioning of the Wise Men, as mentioned in verse 7.

The word *akribos* is also used of Apollos: "This man was instructed in the way of the Lord; and being fervent in the spirit, he spake and taught diligently [*akribos*] the things of the Lord" (Acts 18:25). Here again, the emphasis is not only that Apollos persisted in speaking and teaching the things of the Lord but also that he did so with accuracy. Apollos was able to speak and teach the things of the Lord accurately because he was "mighty in the scriptures" (v. 24). It is possible to persistently speak and teach the things of the Lord without being "mighty in the scriptures," but such a ministry cannot be conducted with accuracy.

The use of the word *akribos* did not mean that Apollos knew everything. The last phrase of verse 25 describes him as "knowing only the baptism of John," which indicates that he had not heard about the coming of the Holy Spirit on the day of Pentecost. Apollos did not have all the Scriptures available to him (very few of the New Testament books had been written); however, he was an able, or capable, student of the Scriptures he *did* have. When Aquila and Priscilla heard Apollos speak, they realized that he needed more information, and "they took him unto them, and expounded unto him the way of God more perfectly [*akribos*]" (v. 26). He already had quite an accurate knowledge about the way of God, but when Aquila and Priscilla shared with him additional information, he learned and was able to speak and to teach even more accurately.

This use of the word *akribos* is also seen in Acts 24:22. The Apostle Paul had given his defense, and "when Felix heard these things, having more perfect [*akribos*] knowledge of that way, he deferred them." Before Paul gave his defense, Felix already knew with some accuracy about Paul and the "way" he represented; but when Paul concluded his defense, Felix knew more exactly Paul's beliefs.

The word *akribos* is also used of believers. Ephesians 5:15 says, "See then that ye walk circumspectly [*akribos*], not as fools, but as wise." The word "circumspectly" means "looking around" or "being cautious." In this instance, *akribos* emphasizes that the believer is to walk accurately, or exactly, because others are watching him. The believer is to be careful how he lives.

The Apostle Paul used the word *akribos* when referring to the knowledge of the Thessalonian believers concerning Christ's Second Coming. Paul told them, ''For yourselves know perfectly [*akribos*] that the day of the Lord so cometh as a thief in the night" (I Thess. 5:2). It was because the Thessalonian believers had an accurate knowledge concerning the Second Coming of the Lord that Paul told them, "But of the times and the seasons, brethren, ye have no need that I write unto you" (v. 1).

Because of their accurate knowledge of the coming of the Lord, they should not be taken by surprise. While some would be taken by surprise and would not escape, Paul told his readers, "But ye, brethren, are not in darkness, that that day should overtake you as a thief" (v. 4).

If we are to have an accurate knowledge about the Lord Jesus Christ and are to be able to speak and teach accurately concerning Him, it is essential that we be "mighty in the scriptures."

Chapter 37

God's Justice Satisfied

When man was created, he was placed in the Garden of Eden and was told that he could freely eat of the fruit of every tree except the tree of the knowledge of good and evil (Gen. 2:16,17). Did he choose God's way or his own way? Man's first sin was that of asserting his will over God's will.

Ever since the first man sinned, the sin nature has been passed on to every descendant. Romans 5:12 refers to this fact: "Wherefore, as by one man sin entered into the world, and death by sin; and so death passed upon all men, for that all have sinned." The greatest proof that every person is a sinner is that he will eventually die. If there had been no sin, there would be no death.

There are two aspects of man's death—physical and spiritual. Physical death occurs when the soul and spirit are separated from the body, and spiritual death occurs when the soul and spirit are separated from God. Sin has already separated every person from God; because of sin, every person born into the world is in a state of condemnation. The question is, How can a person be delivered from condemnation?

Mankind is under God's condemnation because God is perfectly righteous and cannot condone any sin. Yet, because man is hopeless in his state of sin, it is necessary for God to act on man's behalf if man is to be delivered from condemnation. But here the problem arises: How can a perfectly holy God justify, or declare righteous, a sinner? God's perfect righteousness demands justice, but the good news is that God's perfect love provides a way for mercy to be poured out on every sinner.

Referring to Jesus Christ, the Apostle John said, "He is the propitiation for our sins: and not for our's only, but also for the sins of the whole world" (I John 2:2). The Greek word translated "propitiation" is *hilasmos*. This word means "an appeasing, a means of appeasing." When Jesus Christ died on the cross for sinners, His death appeased, or completely satisfied, the Heavenly Father's demands concerning man's sin. Since Jesus Christ took on Himself the form of a man and died on the cross for the sins of the world, God was able to remain completely just, yet He was also able to justify those who believe in Jesus.

The word translated "propitiation" in I John 2:2 is translated the same way in I John 4:10: "Herein is love, not that we loved God, but that he loved us, and sent his Son to be the propitiation for our sins."

A similar Greek word, *hilasterion*, is translated "mercyseat" in Hebrews 9:5: "Over it the cherubims of glory shadowing the mercyseat." In the Old Testament, the mercy seat in the tabernacle, and later in the temple, was sprinkled with atoning blood on the Day of Atonement. This act signified that the Law had been carried out and that God's holy demands had been met. Thus, *hilasterion* refers to the place of propitiation. This word also occurs in Romans 3:25, where it is translated "propitiation": "Whom [Christ] God hath set forth to be a propitiation through faith in his blood, to declare his righteousness for the remission of sins that are past, through the forbearance of God."

On the cross, Christ was both the place of the propitiation and the propitiation itself. He satisfied the demands of God's justice: "To declare, I say, at this time his righteousness: that he might be just, and the justifier of him which believeth in Jesus" (v. 26). Observe from this verse that only those who believe in Jesus are justified.

Another related Greek word, *hilaskomai*, occurs in Hebrews 2:17: "Wherefore in all things it behoved him [Christ] to be made like unto his brethren, that he might be a merciful and faithful high priest in things pertaining to God, to make reconciliation for the sins of the people." Here, *hilaskomai* is translated "to make reconciliation for." Mankind had been separated from God since Adam first sinned, but Jesus' death on the cross made it possible for man to be reconciled to God.

Hilaskomai also occurs in Luke 18:13: "And the publican, standing afar off, would not lift up so much as his eyes unto heaven, but smote upon his breast, saying, God be merciful [*hilaskomai*] to me a sinner." Jesus had not yet died on the cross when the publican prayed this prayer. He actually prayed that God would be propitiated for his sin. This is a prayer that does not need to be prayed now, because Christ has died on the cross and has fully met the demands of God's justice.

145

God has done everything that needs to be done for the sinner. Now it is each person's responsibility to receive Jesus Christ as his personal Saviour. When this is done, the benefits of Christ's death on the cross are applied to that individual. The good news of God's Word is that Christ has paid the penalty for every person's sin. All a man has to do to be delivered from condemnation is to receive Jesus Christ as his personal Saviour. Have you received Christ as your Saviour?

Chapter 38

The Conflict of the Faith

The Scriptures clearly present the truth that salvation is of faith, not of works. The Apostle Paul wrote to believers: "For by grace are ye saved through faith; and that not of yourselves: it is the gift of God: not of works, lest any man should boast" (Eph. 2:8,9).

There is no work that any person can do to contribute to his salvation. A person is saved from condemnation only by placing his faith in Jesus Christ as his personal Saviour.

The Scriptures also say a great deal about the believer's living by faith. Romans 1:17 says, "The just shall live by faith." Colossians 2:6 says, "As ye have therefore received Christ Jesus the Lord, so walk ye in him."

The one who has received Jesus Christ as Saviour is to walk by faith, not by sight. The believer must take God at His Word and live accordingly. For instance, the Bible promises, "If we confess our sins, he is faithful and just to forgive us our sins, and to cleanse us from all unrighteousness" (I John 1:9). The one who walks by faith does not depend on his feelings to tell him when he is forgiven of sin; he depends on the Word of God.

Although the believer has salvation and is to live by faith, this does not mean there is no conflict in the Christian life. Salvation is not attained by struggle but by faith, but there is a conflict which results when one places his faith in Christ.

The Apostle Paul wrote about the conflict he experienced because of the Christian faith. The Greek word he used when referring to this struggle is *agonizomai*, the word from which we get "agonize." *Agonizomai* occurs seven times in the Greek New Testament. Three of these times it is translated by a form of the word "strive" (Luke 13:24; I Cor. 9:25; Col. 1:29). One of its occurrences is translated "labouring fervently" (Col. 4:12). Three times it is translated by a form of the word "fight" (John 18:36; I Tim. 6:12; II Tim. 4:7).

In Paul's time, *agonizomai* and its related words had to do with those who participated in athletic and gladiatorial contests. Thus, it referred to those who were expending all their energies trying to win the prize. Paul brought this word into a Christian context when he applied it to serving the Lord. Paul put forth all his mental and physical energies in serving the Lord, and he exhorted others to do likewise.

To the young pastor Timothy, Paul wrote: "Fight the good fight of faith" (I Tim. 6:12). Literally translated, this phrase reads: "Struggle the good struggle of the faith." This phrase is even more meaningful when the context is considered. Paul had just exhorted Timothy, "But thou,

148

O man of God, flee these things; and follow after righteousness, godliness, faith, love, patience, meekness" (v. 11). Like everyone else, Timothy could acquire salvation only by placing faith in Christ, which he had already done. Much discipline and struggling were necessary if Timothy were to excel in being what he ought to be and in doing the work of the Lord.

The Apostle Paul later wrote to Timothy: "I have fought [*agonizomai*] a good fight" (II Tim. 4:7). As Paul, facing death, wrote these words from prison, he was able to reflect on his life and consider it as already having been finished; thus, he said, "I have finished my course, I have kept the faith" (v. 7).

Although Paul knew the "rest" of faith, which comes to one who realizes what he has in Jesus Christ, he did not decrease the amount of energy he was expending in getting out the gospel to others and in suffering for the cause of the gospel.

We cannot *strive* to be accepted by God, because we are accepted by Him only on the basis of faith (II Cor. 5:9). However, once we have placed our faith in Jesus Christ as Saviour and in all the resources He makes available for daily living, there is a conflict which follows as we expend our energies to win and to teach others.

Chapter 39

Digging Your Own Gems

The Bible is the greatest book that has ever been written. It is the revelation of God Himself. Anyone who wants to understand God must desire to understand the Bible.

However, English readers face a serious problem in trying to understand the Bible. The Bible was written in a different culture and in a different language—the Old Testament in Hebrew (with brief portions in Aramaic) and the New Testament in Greek. To properly understand the message of the Bible, the reader must understand the meanings of its words and how the words were used in the culture of the day in which they were written.

Fortunately, there are tools available to the English reader that enable him to dig below the surface in the Bible and to come up with gems from God's riches. Most of the Bible study aids available are based on the King James Version; therefore, even though you may normally use another translation, you need to know how the word you are studying has been translated in the King James Version. Then you will be able to check the word in various sources, which will help you to understand the significance of the word in the original language.

For serious Bible study, one needs a good concordance to trace every occurrence of the words that appear in the Bible. Such a concordance is *Young's Analytical Concordance to the Bible* (Wm. B. Eerdmans Publishing Co., Grand Rapids, Mich.).* This concordance is especially helpful for a word study, because the reader can easily detect all the verses that use the same Hebrew or Greek word, even though he does not know Hebrew or Greek.

For instance, when one reads in Acts 1:8 that the disciples were promised "power," he can begin a word study by first looking up that word in *Young's Concordance.* As he finds the word "power" and reads down the columns until he comes to the reference Acts 1:8, he will observe that the heading for the group of verses that includes Acts 1:8 is "ability, power." Along with the heading is the Greek spelling and also its spelling in English—*dunamis.* At a glance, you can tell that all of the references that appear under this heading translate the Greek word *dunamis* by the English word "power." By checking several or all of the references and observing their contexts, you will gain valuable knowledge about the shades of meaning intended by this original word, even though you do not know Greek. In order to discover the other ways this same Greek word may be translated in the King James Version, turn to the back of the concordance to the section entitled "Index-Lexicon to the New Testament."

*Recommended books should be purchased from your local bookstore or ordered from the publisher.

By finding the English spelling—*dunamis*—one observes a list of 14 words with a number beside each. These words have each been used to translate the same Greek word in the King James Version. A few of these words are: "ability"—1, "mighty work"—11, "power"—77, etc. This means that this Greek word translated "ability" once in the New Testament is translated "mighty work" 11 times, "power" 77 times, etc. To find where this word is translated in these ways, one would turn back to the main concordance and find the word desired, such as "ability"; then, under the word "ability," he would check the headings until he found the word *dunamis*. The verse under that heading is the one where *dunamis* is translated "ability." By following this procedure for the other translations of *dunamis*, one can trace every occurrence of a Greek word in the New Testament, even though he has never studied Greek.

The procedures for finding the occurrences, the meanings and the various translations of words in the Old Testament are the same as those for the New Testament. There is a section in the back of *Young's Concordance* entitled "Index-Lexicon to the Old Testament," which can be used to find various translations of a particular Hebrew or Aramaic word.

For more information on individual words, one can use the excellent volume, *Expository Dictionary of New Testament Words* by W. E. Vine (Fleming H. Revell Co., Old Tappan, N.J.). By looking up the word "power," one finds a list of all the Greek words (spelled in English) that are translated "power," and comments are given about each. From *Young's Concordance* it was observed that the Greek word in Acts 1:8 translated "power" is *dunamis*. Therefore, one can find the word *dunamis* under the heading "power" in the *Expository Dictionary* and learn more about the use of this word. He will discover that one of the significant shades of meaning of this word is "ability." This shade of meaning is significant in Acts 1:8, because divine ability is precisely what the disciples needed. It was promised to them through the enabling power of the Holy Spirit.

Commentaries written by those who know the original languages are also important to Bible study. Since the same commentary does not appeal to everyone, three commentaries are recommended here. The works of Kenneth S. Wuest have always been much appreciated by English readers who want to know the fine shades of meaning of the Greek. His works are now available in a four-volume set entitled *Wuest's Word Studies from the Greek New Testament* (Wm. B. Eerdmans Publishing Co., Grand Rapids, Mich.). This set is not a commentary on the entire New Testament, but there is other material that the student will find very helpful. Another commentary is *Word Studies in the New Testament* by Marvin R. Vincent (Wm. B. Eerdmans Publishing Co., Grand Rapids, Mich.). This four-volume set covers the entire New Testament, although the author does not comment on every verse.

Another excellent commentary is *Word Pictures in the New Testament* by A. T. Robertson (Broadman Press, Nashville, Tenn.). This commentary gives more technicalities about the grammar of the Greek New Testament. Many of these technicalities would probably be beyond the grasp of one who has not studied Greek. However, this six-volume set on the entire New Testament yields sufficient information to the English reader to make it well worth his investment.

The books recommended in this chapter need not be purchased all at once, but they should be taken into consideration in long-range planning for acquiring Bible study helps.

It must always be remembered that Bible study is *study*. However, you will be thrilled by the jewels you receive from digging out your own gems from the original.

Scripture Index

155

Greek Word Index

KJV Word Index